The Institute of Chartered Financial Analysts Continuing Education Series

Investing in Venture Capital

Washington, D.C.
December 6, 1988

Rodney H. Adams
Tim E. Bliamptis
Katherine A. Cattanach, CFA
T. Bondurant French, CFA
Franklin P. Johnson
Edward W. Kane
C. Kevin Landry

Greta E. Marshall, CFA
Matthias Plum, Jr.
Stanley Pratt
David F. Swensen
Richard J. Testa
Linda A. Vincent

Edited by
Donald E. Fischer, CFA

Sponsored by
The Institute of Chartered
Financial Analysts

Additional copies of this publication may be ordered from

Institute of Chartered Financial Analysts
P.O. Box 3668
Charlottesville, VA 22903
1-804-980-3647
    or
Professional Book Distributors, Inc.
P.O. Box 100120
Roswell, GA 30077
1-800-848-0773

© 1989 The Institute of Chartered Financial Analysts

All rights reserved. No part of this publication may be reproduced, stored in a retrieval system, or transmitted, in any form or by any means, electronic, mechanical, photocopying, recording, or otherwise, without the prior written permission of the copyright holder.

This publication is designed to provide accurate and authoritative information in regard to the subject matter covered. It is sold with the understanding that the publisher is not engaged in rendering legal, accounting, or other professional service. If legal advice or other expert assistance is required, the services of a competent professional should be sought.

From a Declaration of Principles jointly adopted by a Committee of the American Bar Association and a Committee of Publishers.

Katrina F. Sherrerd, *Managing Editor*
Susan S. Brennan, *Production Editor*
Ellen D. Goldlust, *Editorial Assistant*
Joni L. Tomal, *Editorial Assistant*
Diane B. Hamshar, *Administrative Assistant*

ISBN 0-935015-12-4

Printed in the United States of America

Table of Contents

Foreword vii

Biographies of Speakers ix

Overview of the Seminar
    Donald E. Fischer, CFA 1

Introduction
    Matthias Plum, Jr 6

Understanding the Venture Capital Market
    Edward W. Kane 9

Cycles of Venturing
    Katherine A. Cattanach, CFA 15

    Question and Answer Session 20

Setting Realistic Expectations for Potential Returns
    T. Bondurant French, CFA 23
    Linda A. Vincent 26

    Question and Answer Session 31

Valuing Potential Investments
    C. Kevin Landry 32
    Franklin P. Johnson 39

    Question and Answer Session 44

Does Venture Make Sense for the Institutional Investor?
    David F. Swensen 46
    Greta E. Marshall, CFA 52

    Question and Answer Session 55

Terms for Investing
    Richard J. Testa 57
    Tim E. Bliamptis 64

    Question and Answer Session 69

Current Opportunities and Future Prospects
    Stanley Pratt 71
    Rodney H. Adams 76

Panel Question and Answer Session 80

Glossary 84

Self-Evaluation Examination
    Questions 86
    Answers 89

Foreword

The venture capital industry is a relatively small but growing sector of the investable capital market. Many investors have been attracted to this market by the possibility of outstanding returns. These returns, however, are associated with high levels of risk. According to French, venture capital has returned 23 percent compounded per year in the decade 1977-87, with a standard deviation of about 23 percent. Over a longer period, 1959-87, venture capital returns were 15 percent with a 36 percent standard deviation. The industry also has excellent portfolio diversification characteristics; venture displays low correlation with most other asset classes. Because of the characteristics of venture capital, this industry should be of interest to investment professionals.

The Institute of Chartered Financial Analysts sponsored its first seminar on Venture Capital on December 6, 1988, in Washington, D.C. This seminar examined the attractiveness of venture capital as an asset class, with sessions on understanding the venture capital market, cycles that affect venture capital investments, valuing potential investments, setting realistic expectations for potential returns, the terms for investing, whether venture makes sense for institutional investors, and current opportunities and future prospects within the industry. These proceedings are the result of that program.

This seminar brings together an impressive group of professionals who are actively involved in all aspects of venture capital investing. Their shared insights are intended to broaden the reader's perspective into the risks and rewards of a truly dynamic area of investing which is at the heart of innovation and critical to attaining and maintaining commercial leadership and advantage. Their expertise on this subject makes these proceedings a valuable publication. The ICFA wishes to extend its sincere appreciation to Matthias Plum, Jr., Copley Venture Partners who acted as seminar moderator, and to the seminar speakers: Rodney H. Adams, Stanford University; Tim E. Bliamptis, Massachusetts Institute of Technology; Katherine A. Cattanach, CFA, Cattanach & Associates; T. Bondurant French, CFA, First Chicago Investment Advisors; Edward W. Kane, John Hancock Venture Capital Management; Franklin P. Johnson, Asset Management Company; C. Kevin Landry, TA Associates; Greta E. Marshall, CFA, The Marshall Plan; Stanley Pratt, Abbott Capital Management LP; David F. Swensen, Yale University; Richard J. Testa, Esq., Testa, Hurwitz and Thibeault; and Linda A. Vincent, Venture Economics, Inc.

A number of people deserve credit for their contributions to the successful publication of these proceedings. The program was organized by Darwin M. Bayston, CFA, Executive Vice President, and Susan D. Martin, CFA, Vice President—Education and Programs. They received valuable input on the scope of the program from several of the speakers, Rodney H. Adams, Katherine A. Cattanach, and Tim Bliamptis. Tim Bliamptis also contributed the Glossary to the proceedings. Finally, special thanks are extended to Donald E. Fisher, CFA, for editing these proceedings.

Katrina F. Sherrerd
Assistant Vice President
Research and Publications

Biographies of Speakers

Rodney H. Adams is Treasurer of Stanford University. Previously, Mr. Adams served as Director of Finance and Manager of Investments at Stanford, initiated the Stanford Endowment's venture investment program. Mr. Adams serves as Trustee of the Common Fund for Investments, the Treasury Note Trust, the Tax Exempt Trust, and Benham National Tax Exempt Trust. He is a member of the Advisory Committee of Endowment and Foundation Realty Partners, the National Association of University and College Business Officers Investment Committee, the Financial Executives Institute, the Financial Analysts Federation, the Security Analysts of San Francisco, the Financial Management Association, the Western Association of Venture Capitalists, and the Institute for Quantitative Research in Finance. Mr. Adams holds a B.S. and an M.B.A. from Stanford University.

Tim E. Bliamptis is Assistant to the Treasurer of The Massachusetts Institute of Technology. Previously, he was a consultant to the Wharton Small Business Development Center. Mr. Bliamptis has authored numerous technical papers and reports, and has obtained four patents. He holds a B.S. and an M.S. from The Massachusetts Institute of Technology, and an M.B.A. from The Wharton School of Finance of the University of Pennsylvania.

Katherine A. Cattanach, CFA is President of Cattanach & Associates, Ltd. Prior to founding the firm, Dr. Cattanach was Executive Vice President of Captiva Corporation. She is a member of the Board of Directors of Colorado National Bank and Colorado State Board of Education, and a past Commissioner of the Colorado Commission on Higher Education. Dr. Cattanach is also a member of the Region VII Ethics Committee of the Financial Analysts Federation, and past President and a current member of the Board of Directors of the Denver Society of Security Analysts. In addition, she serves on the Board of Directors of the Women's Forum of Colorado. Dr. Cattanach holds a Ph.D. from Arizona State University.

Donald E. Fischer, CFA is Professor of Finance, Graduate School of Business, University of Connecticut. Dr. Fischer is an associate editor of The CFA Digest and has served on the ICFA Council of Examiners (1973-81). He has held positions as management consultant with Deloitte, Haskins & Sells and assistant to the corporate controller, Chrysler Corporation. He is author of *Contemporary Financial Management* (Scott, Foresman), the widely adopted text, *Security Analysis and Portfolio Management* (Prentice-Hall), and numerous articles in the field of investment management.

T. Bondurant French, CFA is Vice President and Senior Venture Capital Advisor of the Venture Capital Division of First Chicago Investment Advisors. Prior to assuming his current position, Mr. French was Head of the Taxable Fixed Income Unit. He has also been associated with Connecticut General. He has lectured frequently on the subject of investment topics and strategies. Mr. French is a member of the Venture Capital Committee, the National Venture Capital Association, the Midwest Venture Capital Association, and the Investment Analysts Society of Chicago. He is also an associate member of the National Association of Small Business Investment Companies. Mr. French holds a B.A. and an M.B.A. from Northwestern University.

Franklin P. Johnson is the Founder of Asset Management Company. Previously, he was Co-Founder of Draper and Johnson Investment Company. Mr. Johnson serves as Chairman of the Board of Boole and Babbage and as a Director of AmGen, Applied Micro Circuits, Coherent, Hypres, Ross Stores, SBE, Tandem Computers, and Teradyne. He is also a Director of the National Venture Capital Association, past President of the Western Association of Venture Capitalists, and a former Trustee of the Foothill-DeAnza Community College District. Mr. Johnson holds a B.S. from Stanford University and an M.B.A. from Harvard University.

Edward W. Kane is Managing General Partner of John Hancock and Co-Founder of John Hancock Venture Capital Management. Previously, Mr. Kane served in the commercial banking division of the Bank of New England. He is a Director of Artificial Intelligence Corp. and Mutual Risk Management, Ltd., and also serves as an advisory committee member of several prominent U.S. and international venture capital funds. Mr. Kane holds a Bachelor's degree from the University of Pennsylvania and a Master's degree from Harvard University Graduate School of Business.

C. Kevin Landry is Managing Partner of TA Associates. Previously, he was a General Partner of the firm. Mr. Landry serves on the Boards of Directors of BTU Engineering Corporation, ImmunoGen, Inc., Softsel Computer Products, Inc., and Standex International Corporation. He is a former Director of numerous companies including Biogen, N.V., Continental Cablevision, Inc., Tandon Corporation, and the National Venture Capital Association. Mr. Landry holds a B.A. from Harvard University and an M.B.A. from the Wharton School of Finance of the University of Pennsylvania.

Greta E. Marshall, CFA is Chief Investment Officer of The Marshall Plan. Previously, Ms. Marshall served as Investment Manager for the California Public Employees' Retirement System, as President of Bay-Banks Investment Management, and as Director of Deere & Company. Ms. Marshall holds a B.A. and an M.B.A. from the University of Louisville.

Matthias Plum, Jr. is General Partner of Copley Venture Partners. Prior to assuming his current position, Mr. Plum was President of Global Investments Limited Partnership. He is a past Chairman of the Financial Analysts Federation, a past Trustee of the Financial Analysts Research Foundation, and a past member of the Education Committee of the Institute of Chartered Financial Analysts. Mr. Plum has also served on the Liberte Advisory Board, as Chairman of the Board of Visitors of the Department of Economics at Boston University, Advisory Board of the Office for the Arts at Harvard and Radcliffe, and as a member of the Corporation of the Museum of Science and Massachusetts General Hospital. He holds a B.A. from Princeton University and an M.B.A. from Harvard University Graduate School of Business.

Stanley E. Pratt is a founding General Partner of Abbott Capital Management, L.P. He is also Chairman of Venture Economics, Inc. Mr. Pratt previously served as Editor and Publisher of *Venture Capital Journal* and as an Editor of *Pratt's Guide to Venture Capital Sources*. He has led seminars for institutional investors and made presentations to government and private sector organizations in the United States, Europe, South America, and Japan. Mr. Pratt is a graduate of Brown University.

David F. Swensen is Associate Vice President of Yale University, where he serves as Chief Investment Officer with responsibility for the Endowment and other investment assets. Prior to joining Yale, Dr. Swensen was Senior Vice President—Corporate Finance at Shearson Lehman Brothers. He is a Fellow of Berkeley College, Yale University and a Trustee of Dwight Hall, Endowment Advisors, Inc., and Endowment Realty Investors, Inc. Dr. Swensen also is a Director of the Investor Responsibility Research Center, Benhaven, and American Development Finance. He is a Founding Member and Executive Committee Member of the International Swap Dealers Association, a Member of the Steering Committee of the South Africa Research Consortium, Chairman and participant in the Interest Rate and Currency Swap Seminars around the world, a Registered Representative of the National Association of Securities Dealers, and a Member of the American Economic Association. He holds a B.S. and a B.A. from the University of Wisconsin—River Falls, and an M.A., an MPHIL, and a Ph.D. from Yale University.

Richard J. Testa is a Partner in the law firm of Testa, Hurwitz & Thibeault. He has served as counsel for several national and international venture capital firms as well as for a large number of high technology and other businesses that have been financed by venture capitalists. Mr. Testa has lectured on numerous legal and financial matters at seminars and continuing legal education programs around the country. He is a graduate of Harvard Law School.

Linda A. Vincent is Vice President of Venture Economics, Inc., where she is Director of Pension Funds Consulting, Venture Capital Fund-Raiser Consulting, and Manager of Institutional Sales. She is also Divisional General Manager of the Investors Services Group, and was instrumental in the organization of the Venture Economics Returns Analysis Program. Prior to joining Venture Economics, Ms. Vincent was a Senior Staff Professional in The Management Consulting Group of Arthur D. Little, Inc. She is a Board Member of the Stanford Business School National Alumni Association, and is a frequent guest speaker at partnership meetings, industry meetings, and conferences. Ms. Vincent holds an A.B. from Cedar Crest College and an M.B.A. from Stanford University, where she was a Chrysler Foundation Fellow.

Overview of the Seminar

Donald E. Fischer, CFA

Venture capitalists are among the principal facilitators of innovation and change in the world. They are angels to the entrepreneur. They solve problems. They create change, value, and wealth. Above all, to achieve success in venture capital investing is to facilitate the entrepreneurial process.

Venture capital is by no means a new arena for investment. Although the current era of venturing is widely believed to date to the founding of American Research and Development Corporation in 1946, the American railroad industry was financed by venture capitalists in the early 1800s.

Venturing has emerged from a fragmented industry dominated by wealthy individuals to an increasingly institutionalized sector where the amount of money committed has skyrocketed. The number of venture firms has increased five-fold in the past ten years—and doubled in the past five years alone. Megafunds have emerged: The idea of raising $100 million funds no longer brings shudders to investors. Most venture capitalists, however, have less than five years experience.

The institutionalization of venture investing has altered the dynamics of the business. More money is chasing available deals. Active involvement with portfolio companies and patience with results may give way to more passive involvement and pressures for performance. Results may be more bimodal in the future—higher returns for some, major disappointments for many others.

This overview merely captures the highlights of the sessions. The presentations are provocative and the question and answer sessions add richness to each session. A glossary is included to facilitate a better understanding of terms peculiar to the art of venture investing.

INTRODUCTION

Matthias Plum, in his opening remarks, describes venture capital as the process of building a business from scratch. He suggests that the typical venture team differs from its public market counterpart, emerging growth stocks, in terms of risk and expected returns, assessment of progress, and difficulty in valuation.

Plum argues that venture capital is linked importantly to innovation. The need for innovation is a critical means for establishing a leadership position in terms of economic activity, exports, and employment. The innovation link is visible within industries as more companies look outside to acquire young enterprises and marry them to existing capabilities to produce and market products.

Plum asks: Are meaningful returns likely from venturing in the future? Venture capital funds started in the 1980s are not tracking prior periods in which 20 to 25 percent returns were the norm. Many people fear further slippage in returns because the supply of funds is outstripping the available deals. Plum questions the observations that funding is excessive.

Plum summarizes what he considers are important issues. First, the effect of inflation should be examined. Inflation has significantly increased the cost of doing business, but not the returns available on that business. Second, new areas of investing are opening all the time. Leveraged buyouts, conglomerate acquisitions, and industry realignments are examples of emerging opportunities. Third, each new deal may require more capital than in the past. The increasing speed of technological progress and the corresponding decrease in time available to market and capitalize on the development is contributing to the increased capital needs.

UNDERSTANDING THE VENTURE CAPITAL MARKET

Edward Kane presents an overview of the venture capital industry. Venture capitalists essentially screen companies, negotiate terms, provide follow-up support to management, and liquidate investment positions. Venturing occurs in stages—start-up through exit—with financing tending to increase as the cycle advances.

Kane suggests that the risks of investing—management, product, market, and operations risks—often characterize the different stages of venture investing. Exit is normally accomplished by the initial public offering of shares or through acquisition.

Kane reminds us that the industry has essentially evolved in two segments: before and after 1980. The periods are distinguished in terms of the type of participants, funds available, and performance. The period since 1980 has seen a dramatic increase in funds available for investment, the emergence of public pension funds as a major provider of funds, and a decline in realized returns.

CYCLES OF VENTURING

Katherine Cattanach describes three cycles in the venture capital industry that impact the investment decision. The first cycle is the portfolio company cycle. The company financed by the venture capitalists (portfolio company) passes through seed, expansion, and mezzanine stages. These companies move from start-up to market introduction to pre-public offering (or merger/acquisition).

Cattanach suggests that there is a second cycle, that of the partnership. The critical aspects of this cycle concern capital flows and valuation. Capital flows include both periodic cash infusions and ultimate distributions. The latter often begin in years three and four and continue off and on up to years seven through twelve. Partnership valuation fits a sort of J-curve when one plots market value against time. Seed values begin to fall below market value, rise with market introduction and expansion, and ultimately level off at liquidation.

The third cycle for venture investing, the environment cycle, refers to cycles in the financial markets, the economy, and political events. The stock market cycle dramatically affects initial public offering opportunities. Economic cycles (recession/expansion) impact both entrepreneurial confidence in start-ups and the degree of caution exhibited by on-line companies. The political cycle embraces such areas as tax policy changes (especially capital gains taxes) and support of Small Business Investment Companies (SBICs).

SETTING REALISTIC EXPECTATIONS FOR POTENTIAL RETURNS

Two speakers, T. Bondurant French and Linda Vincent, discuss the process of setting realistic expectations for potential returns in venture capital investing. They imply that past returns, well above 20 percent, may give way to expected returns in the high teens.

French suggests that venture capital as an asset class is an excellent diversifier in a portfolio. Venture capital displays low correlation (0.10 to 0.35) with public equity, bonds, and real estate. Over a "good" period from 1977 through 1987, venture capital returned 23 percent compounded per annum with a standard deviation of returns also about 23 percent—outdistancing large-capitalization stock returns by over 600 basis points. Over a longer period, 1959-87, venture capital returns were 15 percent with a 36 percent standard deviation.

French suggests that returns should continue to be above average in the future—comparable to results achieved over the past several decades—but not equivalent to the spectacular results of the late 1970s and early 1980s.

Vincent shows that funds begun in the early to mid-1980s are not developing returns at the same rate or levels as funds started in the late 1970s. She also presents return data based on a study of almost 400 companies that had been liquidated (completed full investment cycle) in 13 separate venture funds. Nearly two-thirds of the investments in these funds either lost money or were barely above break-even. Over 15 percent of the investments returned five times or more the invested capital. The losers tend to show up quickly (e.g., in the first 2.5 years) and the big winners took longer; typically they were held five years or more. Vincent reminds us that the pattern of returns is sensitive to the injection of cash, valuations of individual companies, and the timing of distributions.

Vincent notes that a poll of limited partners and investment advisors on future return expectations was almost unanimous in looking for returns in the "high teens." This is in line with French's expected return of 17 percent.

VALUING POTENTIAL INVESTMENTS

In the fifth session, Kevin Landry and Franklin Johnson provide insights into the strategies for valuing potential investments.

Landry argues that potential venture investments should meet some specific tests. First, the management team should be complete and proven. Second, the investment should be in a market with at least $100 million in annual U.S. sales and growth of at least 20 percent per year. Third, competition should be limited.

Landry indicates that his firm seeks a 30 percent compound return on investment overall. They seek to invest mostly where value is rising fastest. This suggests emphasis at the start-up phase, because the price paid is low and the compensation for risk is high. The target here is to make 10 times investment in five to seven years (about a 50 percent internal rate of return). These return targets are sensitive to four key factors: investment price, level of capital required by the businesses, growth rate of specific industries, and the exit price.

The characteristics of success often show that the losers are victims of poor timing (the growth was over). The big winners tend to have leaders with great vision that catch the market just right. For moderate winners, management seems to be the key ingredient.

Johnson indicates that the return performance of venture partnerships must be measured at three levels: the individual investment (portfolio company), partnership, and limited partnership. Johnson reminds us that there are reasons beyond return performance that should also be considered in evaluating an investment. Participation in venture capital provides additional knowledge about emerging industries and companies and generates co-investment opportunities.

Johnson outlines the characteristics to look for in a favorable partnership:

- Are decisions made as a partnership, not as a series of individual entrepreneurs?
- Are partnership funds adequate for its strategy?
- Does the partnership have clearly defined strengths that are emphasized?
- Does the partnership under consideration have good relations with other venture firms?

DOES VENTURE CAPITAL MAKE SENSE FOR THE INSTITUTIONAL INVESTOR?

Does venture capital investing make sense for the institutional investor? David Swensen and Greta Marshall answer with a qualified "Yes." Swensen and Marshall bring experiences from a major endowment fund and a leading public pension fund, respectively, to focus on this question.

Swensen begins by noting that venture capital is considered private equity at Yale University. He identifies three basic characteristics that must be dealt with effectively by any institutional investor in venture: illiquidity, high expected risk and return, and market imperfection. Illiquidity can be tolerated in most endowment portfolios because they typically have a long-term horizon. The high risk-return attributes of venture capital should not be a problem either, although he notes that the risk-return trade-off must be considered within a total portfolio context. Allocating just 10 percent of a portfolio to venture capital can increase return by more than one full percentage point at any given level of risk, according to Swensen.

Market imperfection in venture capital places a premium on company selection. The relative efficiency of the domestic stock market might suggest passive investing as a sensible strategy. According to Swensen, however, a passive approach (allocations to a broad range of opportunities) in the relatively inefficient venture market is a ticket to disaster. Active selection of the best opportunities is paramount.

Swensen's qualified acceptance of venture capital as an asset class is founded on his belief that venture should be viewed within the asset-liability context of a specific institution. Many institutions, however, make investment decisions in venture capital using only historical performance statistics with an increasing lack of patience for results (short time horizons).

In the second part of this session, Marshall discusses whether venture capital makes sense for institutional investors, with an emphasis on the pension funds. She agrees that the illiquid nature of venture capital investments is not a problem because of the long time horizons of pension funds. She suggests a further advantage derived from the fact that venture capital investments are appraised assets. As such, their pricing is not as volatile as that of market-priced portfolios. This difference blends nicely into new pension fund pricing and reporting regulations.

Marshall qualifies her enthusiasm for venture by suggesting caveats to institutional investors based on size of institutions, agency effects, and economic targeting. Even 5 percent of a $50 billion pension fund may exceed total monies committed to the entire venture capital business in one year! It is possible to end up with a very large commitment in a very small industry. Therefore, large size may preclude meaningful participation in venture capital by certain institutions. The agency problem, especially in public pension funds, relates to the asymmetry of return and risk for the manager. The lack of incentive compensation when picking winners—balanced against the potential legislative wrath resulting from bad returns—impacts the types of venture capital funds selected.

Finally, Marshall cautions about economic targeting—setting aside a portion of venture allocation for in-state investing. She believes these restrictions are damaging in terms of the long-term economic consequences to the country.

TERMS FOR INVESTING

The next session discusses the terms used to construct a venture capital partnership. In the first part of the session, Richard Testa outlines the terms that affect partnership returns. In the second part, Tim Bliamptis discusses where we are headed with terms that influence returns received by the limited partners. He then focuses on how these terms impact returns.

Testa notes that the partnership format emerged in the 1960s. The 10-year life partnership is extraordinarily efficient as a business and tax vehicle. The 2.5 percent management fee and the 20 percent carried interest were typical of most partnerships during the 1978-82 upsurge in partnership formations. Today, these terms are being challenged. Management fees are under pressure because the size of funds has increased (e.g., the megafund); the basis for calculating the carried interest is being refined.

Testa suggests that the two-tier partnership is now more common than the traditional single limited partnership. The two-tier structure embraces the main partnership as the investing fund; the general partnership is structured as another limited partnership. The newer structuring is not without its problems. These include issues of vesting, control of operations, dissolution of the firm, and removal of partners.

Testa provides the reader with a detailed summary of the key provisions of a typical limited partnership agreement and discusses some of the issues surrounding each.

According to Bliamptis, the most hotly contested terms relative to their impact on returns are: carried interest, management fees, capital calls, and distribution policies. The standard carry is, and always has been, 20 percent. The management fee has become the most controversial term as the size of funds has increased. In the future, these fees may be based on life of the fund (e.g., first fund vs. follow-on). Capital calls seem to be moving to a system of drawing funds on an as-needed basis (just-in-time funding). Distribution policies are now being driven by the rising importance of institutions in venturing. Here, the trend is clearly toward earlier distribution.

Bliamptis also discusses how terms can impact limited partnership returns. Using a hypothetical fund generating a 52 percent compound return over a three-year period, he shows the following:

- Slowing down the capital calls can add up to 1,000 basis points to returns.
- Lowering the carried interest can add about 400 basis points to returns.
- Cutting the management fee 1 percent can add up to 500 basis points to returns.

Terms do matter!

CURRENT OPPORTUNITIES AND FUTURE PROSPECTS

Stanley Pratt and Rodney Adams conclude the seminar by examining current opportunities and future prospects in venture investing.

In the first part, Pratt tells us that there are some key criteria for successful funds. Obviously, returns are important. The people are also crucial. They must have prior experience as venture capitalists, especially special skills and industry experience. These people must work effectively as a team and exhibit strong judgment. It is imperative that the fund's decision process work for its people and its strategy.

Pratt also discusses current trends in the venture capital industry. Several trends are very important: leveraged buyouts (LBOs), corporate partnering, and international activities. He notes that there is still money to be made in LBOs because they respond to value added from the venture capitalist. Corporate partnering can help add value in more ways than providing money.

International activities—global markets and technology transfers—are an extremely important part of venture capital. Companies worldwide afford opportunities that are not always available in the U.S. infrastructure (e.g., LBOs of family-controlled companies). This LBO process abroad provides the impetus for realignment of capital markets in many foreign countries.

In the second part, Adams discusses the trends in the venture capital industry, including the enormous increase in money and the number of firms committed to venture investing, and the substantial decline in the experience level of people entering the business. Among other key developments in the past few years he suggests:

- Inexperience among investors has fostered "fund-of-funds" entities for deploying capital.
- Both megafunds and dollars-per-deal are on the rise.

- Competition has become very aggressive, resulting in lower returns and less sharing of information.

Adams also offers his opinions of what the future offers:

- lower returns, especially for the very large megafunds and "me-too" syndicators;
- more efforts to get out of venture funds (a developing secondary market);
- desire for more frequent performance reporting, creating undue short-term pressures to produce results; and
- fund managers becoming asset managers because remuneration is geared to management fee income rather than sharing gains.

So what does one do in this evolving environment? Adams suggests participating by using venture fund groups. Once started, be patient. Do not press for performance figures. Be opportunistic in new investments. Cut back on sub-par groups and increase investments in new partnerships of winners.

Introduction

Matthias Plum, Jr.

The venture capital business involves the process of building and financing successful self-sustaining companies, often from scratch. The venture capitalist's responsibility is the active participation in the blending of entrepreneurial insight, capability and desire, sound planning, and strong, experienced management with the necessary capital to enable the development of an ongoing enterprise.

The process takes several years to effect, is no easy task, inevitably meets setbacks along the way, and will call on the capability and talents of venture capitalists, entrepreneurs, and management teams to reach fruition. A successful company will almost by definition prove to be a rewarding investment.

Venture capital investments differ from those of the more familiar emerging growth stock category, which is considered its public market counterpart. In the venture realm, the business risks are usually significantly higher, the assessment of progress more tenuous, and the valuation judgements more difficult. In addition, because of the active participation of the venture capitalists in a company's strategic, personnel, and other policy decisions, the requirements for a successful venture capital management team vary significantly from those usually sought from a manager of public market investments.

The venture capital process serves two important purposes: First, it is a screening device for innovative technologies, products, or services; and second, it is a facilitator for their development. Much has been written about innovation, and yet the ability to foster and capitalize on an innovative effort within a large corporation remains conspicuously elusive and is successful in surprisingly few companies. The reasons for this lack of success are manifold, but they are in part the wellspring of the venture capital process by which innovators and entrepreneurs gain the opportunity to translate their developments into successful products and services.

The venture capital process is important, and innovation is being increasingly recognized as a critical means of attaining and maintaining a leadership position and advantage by developed nations and their indigenous companies. At the political level, this is underscored by the billion-dollar national computer efforts of the 5th Generation in Japan, its counterpart, Esprit, in Europe, and MCC in the United States. The direct national benefits sought after are increased economic activity, exports, and employment. At the corporate level in developed countries, the ability to compete with the newly industrialized countries at the manufacturing level is increasingly in doubt, and companies in the United States and Japan in particular are looking to innovation as the way to preserve their leadership and competitive positions.

It seems reasonable to expect that the need for innovation will rise as more companies perceive its critical strategic importance. History indicates that internal technological development alone will most likely be insufficient to achieve or maintain the desired competitive advantage. Therefore, one can anticipate that large corporate entities will engage in more active participation in, and acquisition of, new technology-based companies to extend their capabilities and leadership. It might be noted that the value of a young enterprise to these corporate acquirers may well be significantly greater than the valuation available from the public market. This is because of the economic advantages of established companies which already have an existing infrastructure through which products can readily be manufactured and marketed with limited, if any, additional capital requirement.

The recognition of the strategic importance of technology and the acquisition of it through corporate partnership arrangements or buyouts is already in evidence. Moreover, we are seeing increased foreign participation in this process as well. From the venture investor's standpoint, this bodes well because it offers an additional exit opportunity for its private company investments at attractive valuations. It also moderates the reliance on the initial public offering route to liquidity, one which is extremely susceptible to the vicissitudes of public market sentiment.

If the basic investment rationale for venture capital remains sound, are there factors which could affect venture investment returns adversely? The answer is "yes". It is increasingly fashionable to believe that venture capital returns will be significantly below their historic norms.

Is this prognostication solidly based? I am not

sure. The concern about future returns is born, in part, of recent experience. In the 1960s, venture rates of return were thought to be in the 20 to 25 percent range. (However, for funds which started in the latter 1960s when the Dow Jones Industrial Average (DJIA) was flirting with the 1000 level and which exited in the mid-1970s when the DJIA was selling near historically low valuations and little more than 50 percent of its prior peak, venture returns, although still positive, were well below those expectations.) With the subsequent rise in price-earnings ratios from 1974 through the early 1980s and a favorable economic environment, partnerships commencing at mid-decade and exiting in the early 1980s had a lot going for them. Internal rates of return in the 35 percent range were not uncommon and, in fact, nurtured the belief that the historic 20 to 25 percent return expectation for venture capital was indeed conservative.

Needless to say, the marketing efforts of a substantial number of new and follow-on venture partnerships in the early 1980s did nothing to allay that expectation. It is not yet possible to be precise about the outcome of partnerships started between 1982-85. Clearly, returns are not "tracking" the prior period, and there is some question whether those partnerships will reach even the historic levels of return.

Although trend extrapolation may contribute to the current forecast of continued slippage of returns from venture capital partnerships that are in the process of being formed at this time, there are several other considerations which contribute to the formation of that conclusion as well:

(1) The five-fold increase in venture capital funding causes some to fear that "too much money is chasing too few deals;"
(2) The proliferation of venture capital groups and people in the industry has lead to increased competition for deals, less networking and support among venture capital partnerships, and decline in the average experience of venture capital "professionals" and teams;
(3) Increased competition for deals affects valuations adversely from the investor's standpoint; and
(4) The larger amount of money to be managed results in less focus on high return, early stage deals which are labor intensive, and more focus on later stage deals which are more capital intensive.

These arguments were summed up by one venture capitalist who said, "Returns will not go up until funding comes down!"

Nonetheless, there are some considerations to be made on the other side of the ledger which may mitigate against the foregoing conclusion. First, inflation has significantly increased the capital cost of developing a new business, but has not reduced the prospective return on investment. The inflation effect represents about half the increase in venture capital funding.

Second, the scope of venture investment activity has broadened greatly, with the result that a significantly lower portion of venture capital funds is now going into traditional venture deals. For example, venture investments are now being made in leveraged buyouts (LBOs), conglomerate acquisitions, and even public securities. Moreover, financial services, savings and loans, and retailing are new areas of opportunity for venture investment.

Taken together, these two factors make one question the extent to which there is an "excessive amount" of venture capital funding available. Moreover, they underscore the ability and willingness of venture capitalists to expand their horizons while seeking to maintain returns.

There are other changes in the fundamental practice of the venture capital business which bear their issue. The quickening pace of technological progress and the corresponding diminution in the time available to capitalize on new developments increase capital requirements for start-up companies. For example, in the computer industry in the early 1980s it took roughly $30 million to develop a parallel processing company and four years to reach revenues in excess of $50 million. In the late 1950s it took Digital Equipment less than $100,000 in equity and $1 million in debt to reach half that level of volume. It also took more than a decade.

The net result is that the risks are higher because of the greater capital commitment and the "shorter window of opportunity." On the other hand, the rewards for success are greater because of the large niche markets available, and the ability for the successful company to become sizeable and liquid in a shorter time frame.

Venture fund size has increased, often without a commensurate increase in experienced personnel. Because of the heavy time requirement in seed-stage deals and the corresponding limited amount of capital needed at that level, there is more focus on and interest in later stage investment. This may reduce the "average risk level" of the overall venture industry or a particular partnership. Theory would lead one to expect a corresponding diminution in the rate of return. However, to the extent that may occur, a prospective investor may take active steps to rebalance the risk through judicious selection of the mix of venture partnerships, including some partnerships that focus more heavily on seed- and early-stage investments.

Finally, there is a phenomenon that may bode well for rates of returns for today's venture investor. The venture industry tends to look to public market valuations as a proxy for exit prices for venture investments. Although one tends to normalize these expectations, the nature of venture investment as a continuum makes practice and theory diverge. Mezzanine (last private round) financing tends to be influenced heavily by current public market conditions. This in turn affects second-stage valuations, which impact those of first-stage investments. Thus, market prices affect all stages of venture valuations to some degree.

Currently, the public market serves to reduce venture expectations (and, hence, valuation) in two ways. Today, receptivity of the public market to initial public offerings (IPOs) is low, less than one-third of the 1986 level. With IPO market availability severely curtailed, the perceived length of the holding period and private capital requirements of venture investment have been increased. Moreover, the valuation (as measured by relative price-earning ratios) being accorded the emerging growth company sector of the public market is historically low. Taken together, these factors are depressing the valuations that venture investors are willing to place on their new investments.

However, should public market conditions return to more normal levels, exit valuations should increase substantially. Moreover, exit opportunities would be facilitated by greater market receptivity to IPOs. Thus, the opportunity for increased liquidity at significantly higher levels of valuation without relying on above average market conditions is a distinct possibility. Should normal market conditions recur, investment returns for the venture investor would prove attractive and reach or even exceed the historic 20 to 25 percent range.

It may be worth noting that the vicissitudes of the public market coupled with the long-term nature of venture investment argue strongly for a program of continuous commitment to the venture segment of a portfolio. This is an approach which bears its public market analog in "dollar price averaging" and is a means of eliminating the variability associated with investment in trough-to-peak and peak-to-trough market time frames. For the institutional investor, this strategy should be appropriate if the underlying average return is deemed to be attractive.

This discussion of alternative assessments of the current venture capital scene is presented as a backdrop to the presentations that lie ahead. Given the controversial outlook for venture capital, I hope that you will approach the presentations in this book with both a receptive and skeptical frame of mind.

Understanding the Venture Capital Market

Edward W. Kane

In this presentation, I will provide an overview of the venture capital industry. Just as fire needs three elements for combustion, the venture capital industry needs three ingredients to be successful: the investors (the fuel), the venture capitalists (the oxygen—think of this as the catalyst), and the entrepreneurial companies (the heat). This relation is illustrated in Figure 1.

THE VENTURE CAPITALIST

The role of the venture capitalist is important. The venture capitalist must: (1) screen potential investment opportunities; (2) analyze the potential companies and their industries; (3) negotiate the terms of specific transactions; (4) provide follow-on support to management; and (5) liquidate investment positions.

The term "deal flow" refers to the process of sourcing and screening potential investment opportunities. This term is sometimes misleading. It implies that a venture capitalist sits at a desk as a flow of deals comes at him and he selects opportunities in which to invest. Rather, a good venture capitalist will search out and create investment opportunities, much as a prospector pans for gold.

The other roles of a venture capitalist are self-explanatory. Several points are worth noting, however. First, the follow-on support to management is a key role. Second, liquidations of the investment position are handled differently by the traditional venture capitalists and fund-of-funds managers. Generally, a traditional venture capitalist distributes stock to his investors in the form of restricted securities. Typically, there is a holding period required before these securities can be sold, and there is a legend on the securities containing restrictions. A fund-of-funds manager will first make the decision on whether to hold that stock or sell it; if he decides to sell it, he must then decide when and at what price. Sometimes a fund-of-funds manager can remove restrictive legends associated with those securities and file the forms that are necessary to make the securities liquid for the investor. Thus, in most cases, a traditional venture capitalist returns securities, and a fund-of-funds manager returns cash.

STAGES OF VENTURE INVESTING

Figure 2 shows the stages of venture investing. Over time, the intrinsic value of a portfolio company increases. The stages begin with a seed investment, generally made when there are one or two people in the company; the investment is a small amount intended to finance development of the concept or the business plan. The seed investment is generally less than $1 million and frequently can be less than $500,000.

The start-up round is generally the first real venture capital round. This financing is in the range of $1 to $2 million, and there is normally a syndicate of investors participating. If the investment is in a capital-intensive industry, the financing may be greater than $2 million. The venture capital investors get about 50 percent of the company in return for the amount of capital invested and the management gets the other half. So if it is a $2 million financing, the pre-money valuation is $2 million and the post-money valuation is $4 million.

The early-stage financing generally involves a larger round of financing—typically in the range of $4 to $6 million. There are several terms used to describe the phases of the early stages of development. The "bread board" is when the product is in its initial stages, but not quite put together. "Alpha site" is when the first unit of product has been built but has not been shipped (however, it is usually operating on the company's premises). "Beta site" is when the product has been placed in the hands of a user; it is usually a friendly user—a corporation which has agreed to serve as a beta site and use this product to see if it can make a go of it. Everyone knows that the product is not finished; it will need further engineering. At this stage, the team is in place and all the management positions have been filled.

The expansion financing stage is often a $5 to $15

FIGURE 1. Ingredients of the Venture Capital Market

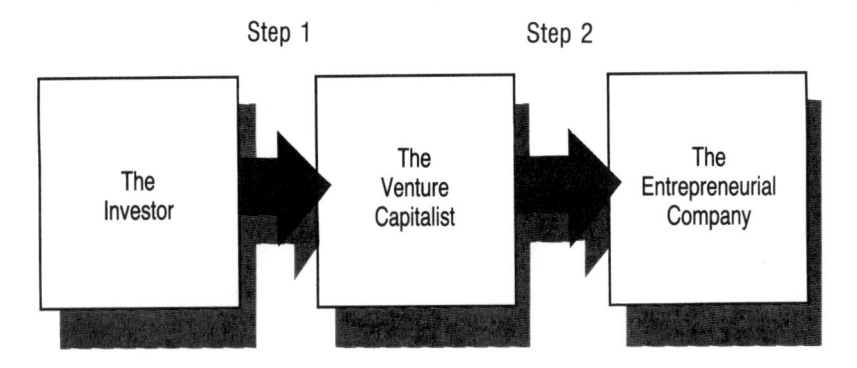

The Investor → Step 1 → The Venture Capitalist → Step 2 → The Entrepreneurial Company

Source: John Hancock Venture Capital Management

million round of financing. At this point, the company is approaching profitability, and execution risk is a key factor. The company is shipping products at a rate of about $1 million a month, and is either profitable or approaching the break-even point.

The later stage, or bridge financing, is a $10 to $20 million round of financing. The company is usually profitable at this stage. This round is often in lieu of an initial public offering (IPO). (In 1983, this stage was nicknamed "gangplank financings" because the IPO marketplace disappeared.) The makings of a real company are apparent and if the IPO market is nonexistent, a later stage or bridge financing occurs if the company needs capital.

Leveraged buyouts (LBOs) are an alternate exit opportunity. From a venture capitalist's point of view, an LBO is not always an option because it usually is only viable in a mature industry, and the return frequently comes from the financial architecture involved and not necessarily the growth of the company.

THE EVOLUTION OF THE VENTURE CAPITAL INDUSTRY

The evolution of the venture capital industry may be separated into two segments: before and after 1980. Figure 3 illustrates the evolution of the venture capital industry. Prior to 1980, venture capital was

FIGURE 2. Stages of Corporate Development/Rounds of Venture Financing

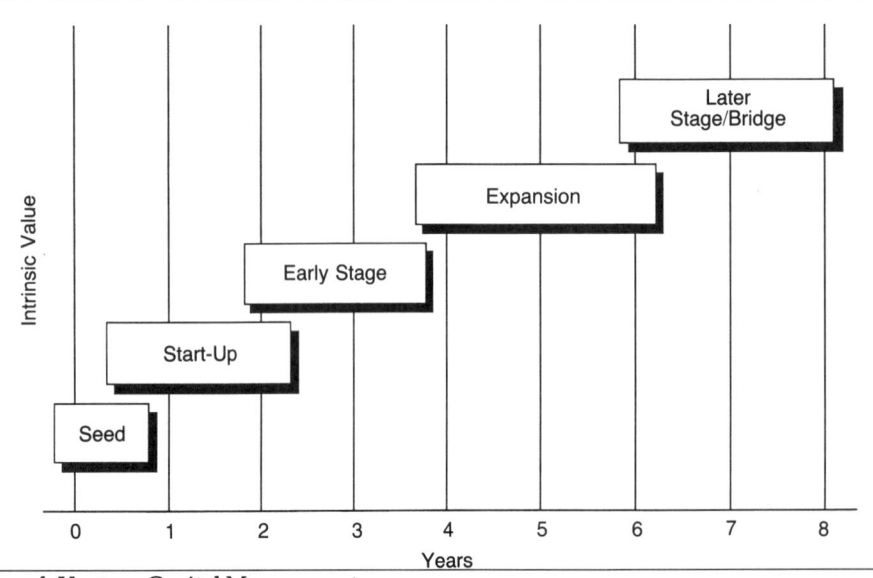

[Chart showing Intrinsic Value vs Years (0-8), with stages: Seed, Start-Up, Early Stage, Expansion, Later Stage/Bridge]

Source: John Hancock Venture Capital Management

really a cottage industry. Its history can be traced back to pre-revolutionary days. For example, there were two venture capital investments done in Massachusetts before 1800: the Saugus Ironworks in about 1645 and the Middlesex Canal in about 1789.

Prior to the late 1940s, individuals and families were the primary source of capital. The founding of American Research and Development in 1946 launched the venture capital fund as we use the term today. American Research and Development made the initial investment into Digital Equipment Corporation, which was a hugely successful investment.

From the 1960s to the late 1970s, the venture capital market was largely the domain of insurance companies and foreign investors. Pension funds were not in the venture capital industry before the 1980s in part because venture capital was not considered to be a prudent investment. Venture capital is now considered a prudent investment. As a consequence, in the late 1980s, public pension funds participated actively in the venture capital market.

The venture capital industry has grown rapidly since 1978. Figure 4 shows that in the early 1980s, the industry absorbed much more capital than it did in the late 1970s. The banner year for venture capital was 1983, in which commitments jumped to $3.4 billion. This surge is correlated with a very healthy—some would argue frothy—public securities environment for technology stocks. Since then, the funding level has remained relatively stable. Table 1 shows the sources of capital commitments from 1983 to 1987. It is interesting to note the increasing role that public pension funds are playing. Foreign investors and corporations have remained relatively stable as a funding source. Table 2 shows that public pension plans are expected to provide about 20 percent of the capital in the future, up from only 12 percent in 1987. The participation of other groups will remain about the same.

Figure 5 shows geographically the involvement of public funds in venture capital. The industry has tended to be bicoastal, and most of the venture capital investing has occurred in the northern part of the country. There is a noticeable lack of capital coming from the Southeast. That is not to say that there are not investment opportunities and a number of attractive companies in the Southeast; it simply means that the Southeast has not yet reached the critical mass that has occurred in the Northeast and the Midwest and, to some extent, the Pacific Northwest.

RISK-REWARD CHARACTERISTICS

The risk-reward characteristics of a venture capital investment are straightforward. There are four types of risk—management, product, market, and operations risk—and the potential for substantial returns. The management risk is that the team will not be able to work together. One must assess whether the chemistry is right, whether the people get along, and whether the company will be able to meet its payroll. Frequently, members of the management team are changed—perhaps as many

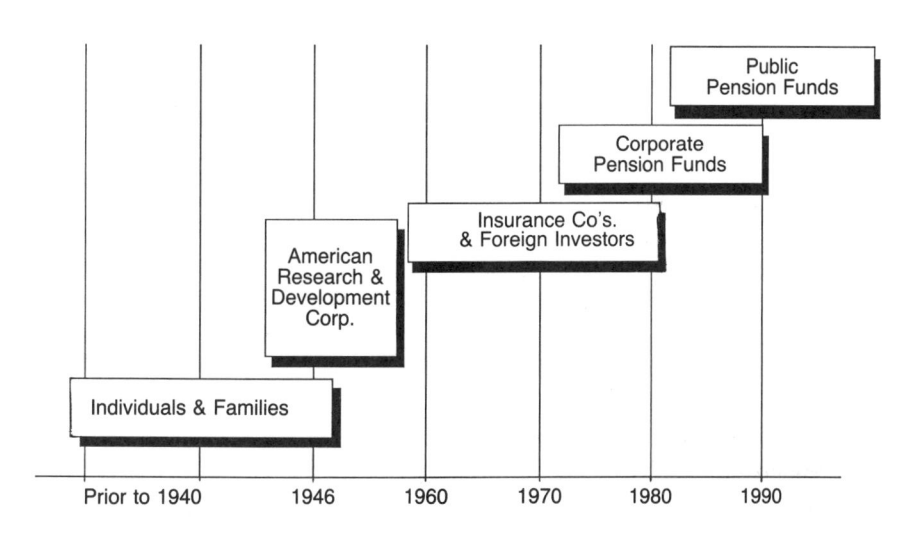

FIGURE 3. Evolution of the Venture Capital Industry

Source: John Hancock Venture Capital Management

FIGURE 4. Capital Commitments to Independent Private Funds 1978-1987

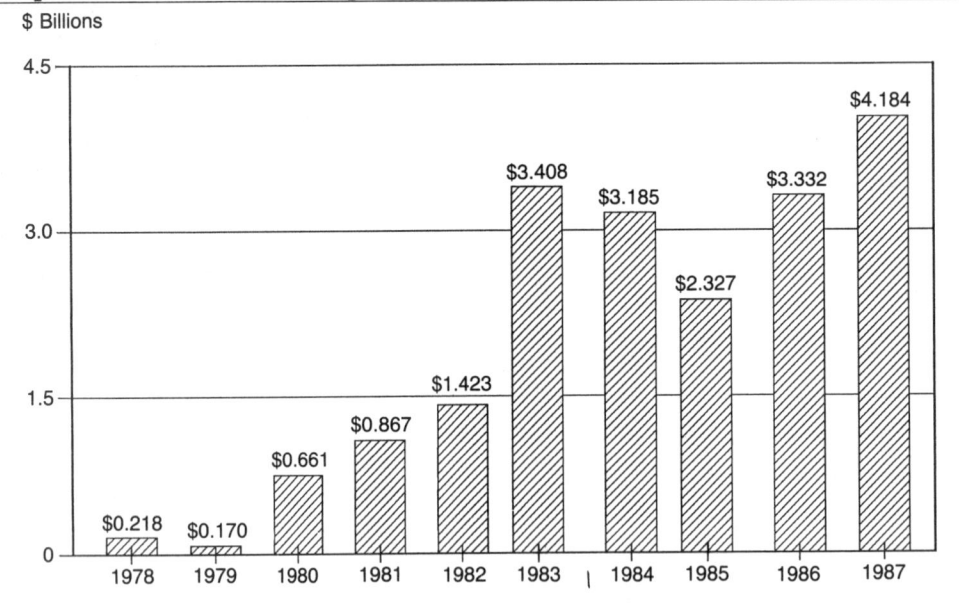

$ Billions

1978	$0.218
1979	$0.170
1980	$0.661
1981	$0.867
1982	$1.423
1983	$3.408
1984	$3.185
1985	$2.327
1986	$3.332
1987	$4.184

Source: Venture Economics

as three times on the way to a successful investment. This is the most critical risk that is taken by the investor.

Investors should also be concerned about product risk. Whatever is being developed, whatever is being created—can it be made to work? A lot of money is poured into companies where the products simply do not work. That is not a flaw—failure is an intrinsic part of this industry. Nonetheless, it is a risk that venture capitalists take on and it needs to be addressed.

The third risk is market risk. Will the market accept the product? A company may have a very coherent management team and a product that works fabulously—but nobody wants to buy it. This is one of the major frustrations with the venture capital industry. Obviously, significant losses are incurred in these instances.

The fourth risk is the operations risk—quality control. Can the company produce its product in volume? It is not enough to be able to produce one or two of these things. The company must be able to roll them out, raise the gross margins, and reduce the product costs. One of the fundamental issues facing the venture capital industry is the whole issue of cost reduction, particularly because the country must compete with foreign sources of manufacturing.

If these four risk factors are combined before the company runs out of money, and if everything comes together at the same time, then the potential exists for very substantial rewards. If these companies are not up and running quickly, they will get knocked out of the box by a competitor, or they will run out of financial resources.

TABLE 1. Sources of Capital Commitments: Independent Private Funds (in millions of dollars)

	1983	1984	1985	1986	1987
Public Pension Plans	$ 162	$ 300	$ 220	$ 89	$ 500
Corporate Pension Funds	895	785	547	1,283	1,132
Individuals & Families	715	467	303	392	502
Foreign Investors	545	573	548	361	544
Corporations	409	463	274	350	460
Insurance Companies	409	419	254	348	628
Endowments & Foundations	273	178	181	209	418
Total	$3,408	$3,185	$2,327	$3,332	$4,184

Source: Venture Economics

TABLE 2. Sources of Capital Commitments: Independent Private Funds

	1987	1988 (Proj.)
Public Pension Plans	12%	20%
Corporate Pension Funds	27%	28%
Individuals & Families	12%	11%
Foreign Investors	13%	11%
Corporations	11%	10%
Insurance Companies	15%	9%
Endowments & Foundations	10%	11%
Total	100%	100%

Source: John Hancock Venture Capital Management

CHARACTERISTICS OF A VENTURE CAPITAL INVESTMENT

Venture capital investments have unique characteristics. First, it is a long-term investment process: It takes a lot of time to build a successful company. Second, to be successful, companies often need to change managements and/or products. If a product does not work, the company may have to change its configuration. Or it might have developed the right product for the wrong market and have to change its market focus. Frequently, additional rounds of financing are necessary when these changes are required.

The long-term nature of the industry is evident at the liquidation phase. There are two routes to liquidating an investment: IPO or acquisition. The median age of a venture-backed IPO and the median age of a venture-backed acquired company are both five years. Frequently, even after an IPO, there are restrictions on the stock that limit its liquidity. For example, even though a company is public and beyond the two- or three-year holding period under SEC Rule 144, one might not be allowed to sell the stock because of restrictions imposed during negotiations between the investment bankers, the company, and the investors. This is yet another example of the long-term nature of the industry.

In the venture capital industry, there are two performance characteristics that should be highlighted: (1) losers tend to appear more quickly than winners, and (2) portfolio companies are usually valued conservatively. These characteristics underlie the J-curve.

The nature of the industry is such that there is a conservative bias built into the valuation techniques for venture capitalists. Typically, investments are carried at cost, written down as performance dictates, and written up only after significant third-party transactions. With a few minor exceptions, there is amazing consistency in this industry. The inconsistencies often result from timing differences in the preparation of the financial statements for a particular partnership. These differences usually last only one quarter before the discrepancy is corrected. By being conservative, a partnership might take a write-down if the company's performance deteriorates, but would not then write it up if the company's performance is very good. If

FIGURE 5. Public Funds in Venture Capital

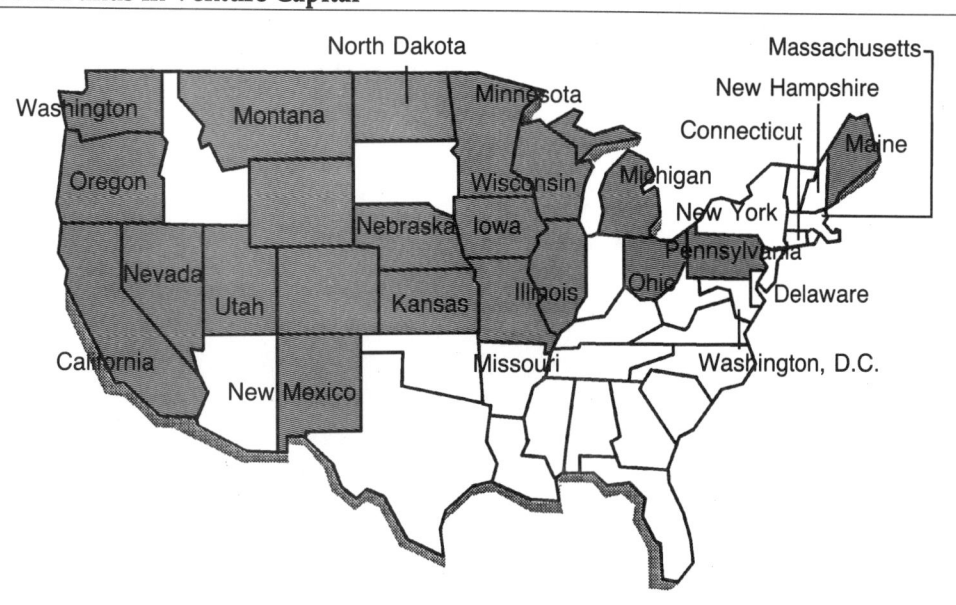

Source: John Hancock Venture Capital Management

FIGURE 6. Venture Portfolio Company Returns: A 218-Company Survey

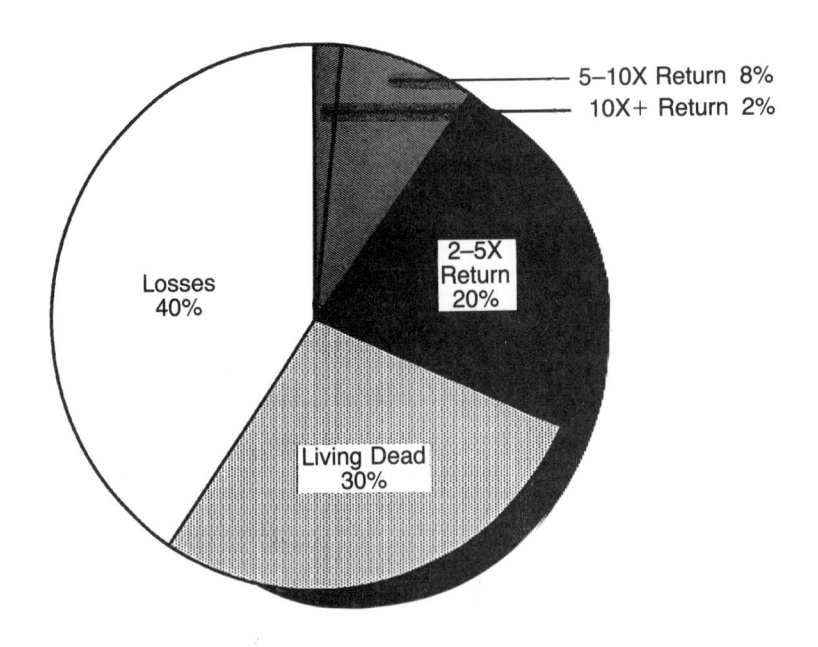

Source: Venture Economics

the company meets its business plan, turns profitable, receives solicitations from investment bankers, and there is a lot of interest in acquiring the company at a favorable price, one still would not write that company up until an event has occurred.

The performance of venture investments covers a broad spectrum. Figure 6 shows the results of a survey of investment performance. Almost half of the companies, or 40 percent, result in partial or total losses to the portfolio. Another 30 percent of the investments are referred to as "living dead." These are companies that move sideways—they consume a lot of time and management energy and do not make much money. Another 20 percent of the investments are referred to as "two- to five-times winners" (i.e., return is two to five times invested capital). The last 10 percent of the portfolio generates the most satisfaction because about 8 percent of the portfolio has the potential to provide five- to ten-times return and 2 percent of the portfolio provides returns in excess of 10 times. These are the kinds of returns that make the venture capital industry what it is. The win-loss structure is analogous to a 100-story skyscraper: the profit for the whole project is going to come out of the top two floors.

Cycles of Venturing

Katherine A. Cattanach, CFA

There are four cycles in the venture capital industry: (1) portfolio firm cycles; (2) partnership cycles; (3) market, economic, and political cycles; and (4) the venture investing cycle. In this presentation, I will describe these cycles and show how they influence the investment decision. But first, let us define a couple of the terms we will be using. The portfolio company is the company backed or financed by venture capitalists. The venture capitalist(s) will provide not only needed capital but management, marketing, and sometimes product consulting. This assistance can help the firm through the early growth period when it is struggling to become a viable, commercially successful entity to the point where it is either sold or taken public through an initial public offering (IPO).

The venture capital partnership or fund is normally a portfolio of 20 to 30 investments in venture capital companies. The partnership or fund is run by venture capitalists, the general partners of the firm. This is the investment vehicle used by most institutional investors for investing in venture capital.

PORTFOLIO FIRM CYCLES

With a few modifications, the traditional life cycle concept may be applied to a portfolio company within a venture capital partnership. First, the life cycle of a portfolio company is truncated in the sense that it ends when the portfolio company exits from the partnership portfolio; the life cycle is not normally beyond the point of distribution to the investors. Second, the life cycle of the portfolio company is described in terms of its funding stages rather than the more traditional life cycle characteristics of development of management, objectives, growth, and profitability. Those funding cycles do, however, generally correspond with traditional developmental milestones.

Let us look at the model of the portfolio company life cycle in Figure 1. There are three major phases: start-up, expansion, and mezzanine. The start-up or seed phase is the initial innovative idea period during which the entrepreneur(s) flesh out the basic concept that underlies the company's reason to be, its strategic advantage. Often, the beginning of this phase is a time of limited management team capabilities. Generally, the company has only one or two employees—the entrepreneurs with the basic idea. Objectives at this point in the company's life include developing a comprehensive business plan, hiring a management team, and proving that the concept is viable or that the prototype works and meets customer needs.

The second stage is the expansion phase. This is an adolescent period in the company's life cycle, a time of market introduction. During this phase, the company must analyze the competition and the marketplace based on real world feedback. Even a good idea can fail because of either competitive pressures or an inhospitable marketplace. Both marketing and sales must function with product development that meets the needs of actual customers. This is also the time when a cohesive management team must be developed. In many cases, the entrepreneur is not the right person to take the company forward to commercial viability; this possibility must be addressed as soon as it is evident. The primary objective during this period is to prove market acceptance. A frequently used benchmark is whether the firm has the ability to generate $5 to $10 million in annual sales and to reach profitability.

The third phase of the portfolio company life cycle is the mezzanine stage, also referred to as later stage or bridge stage. It is the pre-public-offering or the pre-merger/acquisition period in the company's life. Sometimes, if the IPO market is very active, the company may not need this final round of venture funding. Objectives during this phase are to build a stable, experienced management team. This team should be one that can carry the firm to the post-venture period, generate a sustained product or service for market penetration, and demonstrate a family of follow-on products or services. Very few companies can make it in the real world with only one product or one service. Survival depends on a family of products that fit together cohesively. The company also needs a strategy that demonstrates a financial annuity, customer relations, leverageable technology, and so forth. Finally, the company must demonstrate its ability to sustain profitability and financial stability.

FIGURE 1. Portfolio Company Life Cycle

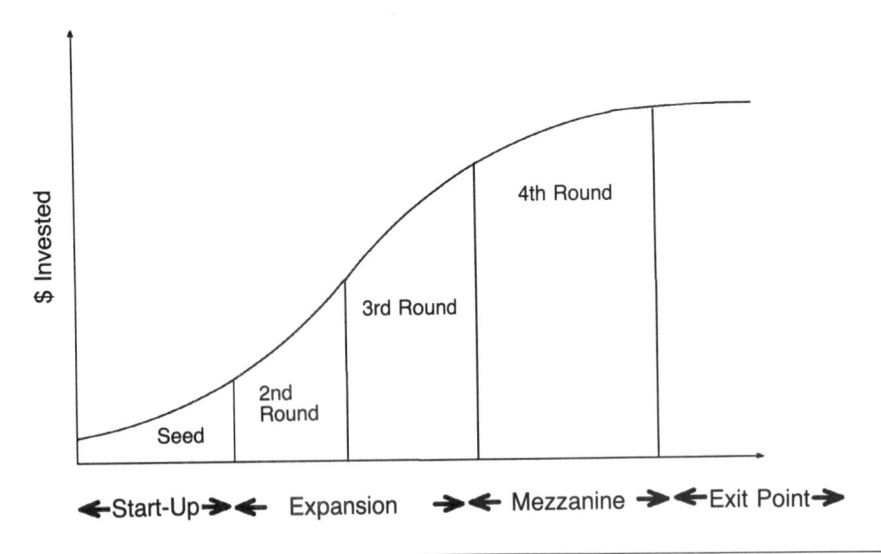

Source: Cattanach & Associates

PARTNERSHIP CYCLES

There are three aspects of the venture capital partnership life cycle: (1) capital flows; (2) valuation; and (3) management. The first two aspects pertain to each individual partnership. The management aspect pertains to the general partnership (the venture capitalists or general partners) which may manage several individual partnerships.

Capital flow may be divided into two subcycles—the call cycle and the distribution cycle—as depicted in Figure 2. The call cycle is the period of time during which the investors' money which has been committed to the partnership is called down by the general partners. Calls may come on a regularly scheduled basis; e.g., one-quarter of the commitment at closing and another quarter on each of the first three anniversaries. However, the industry is moving increasingly to investors providing 10 to 20 percent of the capital committed at closing, and the rest on an as-needed basis, with a 30-day notice. In this case, the general partner would only call the

FIGURE 2. Venture Capital Partnership Life Cycle

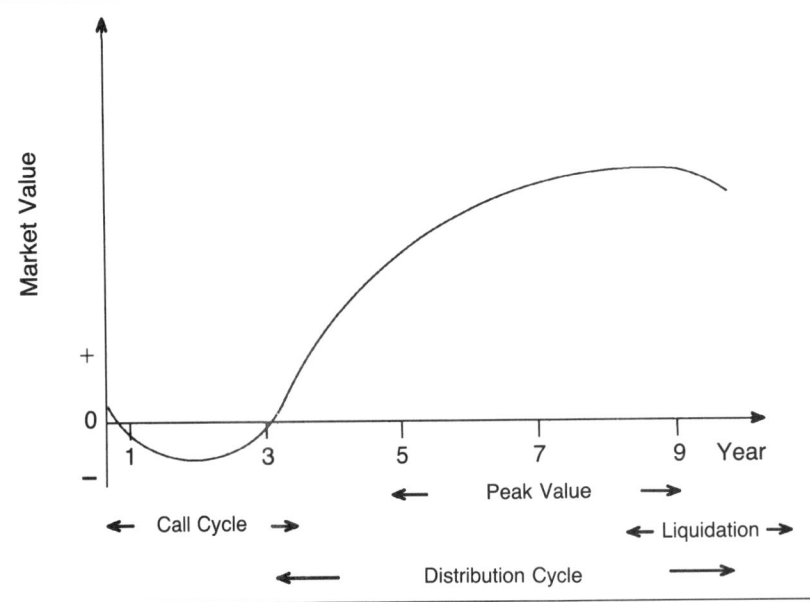

Source: Cattanach & Associates

funds when he or she is ready to invest.

Capital infusions are used for two purposes: investments in new portfolio companies and follow-on investments. General partners often invest in follow-on, or later-stage, rounds, both in their own companies and in companies based in other partnerships. The latter insures diversification and cements relations with other venture capital groups. This is particularly important because the venture capital industry operates very much on a quid *pro quo* basis. This posture is akin to saying, "You show me your good deals and I will show you mine."

Returns are realized by investors in the form of stocks or cash during the distribution cycle. For most funds, distributions begin in years three and four, and continue for the remainder of the partnership, generally seven to twelve years. The pattern of distributions for each partnership will depend both on the investment strategy of the fund and on financial market conditions. Thus, a start-up fund may not begin making distributions until year five, six, or even seven, because distributions occur when the portfolio companies mature and are ready for a public offering or for a merger/acquisition. If a fund specializes in later-stage companies, the distribution cycle generally begins much earlier, because initial investments in a particular company will have been made when that company is more mature and therefore closer to the exit point.

Partnership valuation generally fits a pattern called the J-curve, as illustrated by the curved line in Figure 2. The reported value of a fund is frequently less than the amount of money committed to that fund during the early years. This pattern occurs because portfolio losers tend to show up much earlier than the successful investments, which take time to mature. Typically, the losers are written off as quickly as possible, which causes the value of the fund to fall. In addition, a management fee must be paid out of committed capital, further reducing the value of the fund, which is particularly noticeable in the early years before value begins to build in portfolio companies.

As it matures, the partnership increases in value because the successful portfolio companies are increasing in value. On average, the peak value period for a partnership occurs between years five and nine. Distributions will be made during that period, thus reducing remaining partnership value. But there is unrealized value in the portfolio, reflecting the underlying value of companies still held in the portfolio. In the liquidation phase (years eight through ten), cumulative distributions become larger and the value remaining in the fund becomes commensurately smaller. Finally, there is often a one- to three-year wrap-up period at the end of a partnership's life to tie up the loose ends in the portfolio.

General partnerships (the managers of the venture capital partnerships) also have a life cycle. Figure 3 illustrates the progression of funds over time. Frequently, there will only be one or two general partners with a first fund (Fund I). They may

FIGURE 3. Management Phases

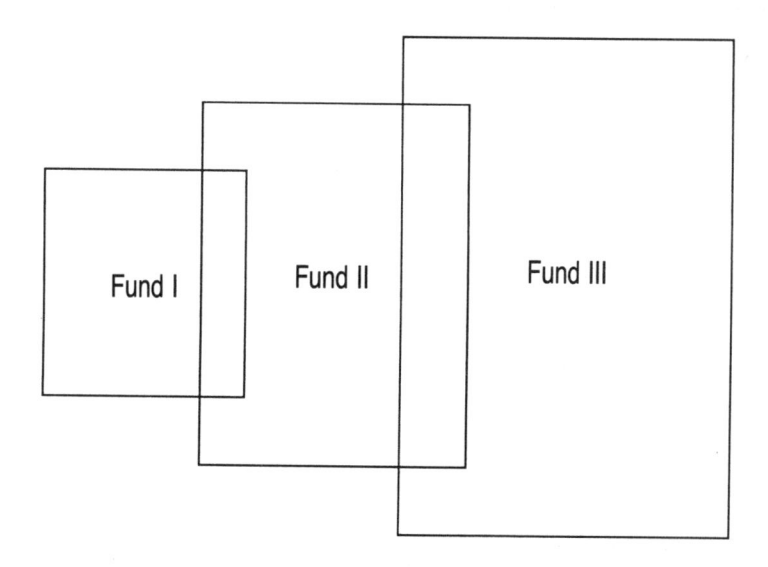

Source: Cattanach & Associates

have operating backgrounds, or they may have worked with another venture capital partnership. They will have convinced a group of investors that their background is sufficient to manage successfully a new venture capital partnership. As a rule, these early funds operate with a relatively small amount of money.

By the third or fourth year most of the money that has been committed to the first partnership will have been invested in, or committed to, portfolio companies, with approximately 30 percent of the capital reserved for follow-on funding for specific portfolio companies. Once the capital has been committed to portfolio companies, the partners begin to think in terms of raising additional capital for a second fund, a follow-on fund. Generally, because there is now at least the beginning of a track record and the economics are more favorable, the follow-on fund will be larger (Fund II). Typically one or two general partners and an associate or two are added. Thus, the second fund exhibits a more mature general or managing partnership structure than the earlier fund. With the addition of more money, the partners have greater financial leverage.

This pattern repeats itself. In the third or fourth year of Fund II, when the general partners have committed the funds of the second partnership, they will start the fund-raising process for yet another follow-on fund.

At this point we begin to see what is being called the institutionalization of partnerships, when the general partnership resembles a financial institution more than the entrepreneurial entity characteristic of early venture capital partnerships. These more mature venture organizations may have a structure which includes general partners, junior partners, associates, and several levels of management. Frequently, there is also a pattern of specialization. Instead of working together on every single investment, partners will divide into teams, sometimes operating in different offices where they may specialize by geography, technology, or some other criteria. Around this time, many of the founding general partners begin to withdraw from the day-to-day activities of running the funds. Sometimes they are tired. This is a very high-risk, high-intensity kind of business. Often they have made more than enough money to satisfy their needs for the rest of their lives.

MARKET, ECONOMIC, AND POLITICAL CYCLES

Cycles in the stock market, the economy, and the political environment also have a decided impact on the venture capital industry. Clearly, the impact of the stock market on the venture industry is direct and dramatic. It affects both pricing and the availability of capital. For example, between 1973 and 1983 there was an increasing amount of money available for venture capital. It was a very enticing investment: returns were exciting, the stock market was hot, and everybody wanted to get on board—so the money became available. As a result, the price of venture capital deals increased dramatically, and it became more difficult to earn outstanding returns. The cycle continues: today prices on venture capital deals are coming down. The small capitalization segment of the market is near an all-time low as reflected in the price-earnings ratio of T. Rowe Price's New Horizon Fund relative to that of the S&P 500. Demand has diminished. The market is not quite so enamored with venture capital as it was.

Opportunities for venture investing often parallel the stock market. Various segments of the industry become more or less profitable over time. Historically, the venture environment favored investments in high technology, biotechnology, medical products, data communications, and the computer industry as the foundation for returns. More recently, other sectors such as retailing and financial services have become important. These rotations are similar to rotation patterns in the stock market.

Finally, of course, the stock market environment affects exit opportunities. It is very hard to have an IPO if there is no IPO window. So when the market shuts down, the IPO opportunity for exiting evaporates and venture capitalists must provide additional financing to carry their portfolio companies until they can be financially self-sufficient. In poor IPO markets, mergers and acquisitions often become the only attractive exit options.

Economic cycles also have an impact on the venture capital industry. There is a strong correlation between entrepreneurial confidence and what is happening in the economy. When the economy is thriving, people are willing to take risks; they are willing to leave their jobs to try out their ideas. When the economy goes into a recessionary slump, or when there is tremendous uncertainty about what is going to happen, potential entrepreneurs pull back. They become concerned about whether they will be able to find a good job if their idea is not viable. Of course, when the economy is doing well, companies which have progressed to actual sales do relatively well if they have a viable product which is being correctly marketed.

Conversely, when the economy is in a recession, even excellent companies have to pull back and conserve cash. In these ways, the economy has both a psychological and a tangible impact on the venture capital industry.

Foreign strategic investors in venture capital may be affected less by the U.S. economy than American investors. They tend to be longer-term investors who are more interested in looking at the window of opportunity for co-investing than the short-term cycle. Exchange rates also have an impact on the attractiveness of the U.S. venture capital market to foreign investors, although it is often a secondary rather than a primary factor. In fact, foreign investors are probably influenced more by economic cyclicality in their own economies.

Venture capital opportunities differ by region. Both Boston and the San Francisco Bay area have a wonderful infrastructure for venture capital investing. Historically, Boston has been known for midrange computer and software companies; the Silicon Valley, for computer hardware. These distinctions are, however, becoming less clear over time. Other regions of the country have been less attractive, although there are pockets of opportunity in the Northwest, the Rocky Mountains, Texas, and the Research Triangle regions.

Finally, political cycles can affect the venture capital industry. For example, many people believe that the reduction of the capital gains tax rate to 28 percent in 1978 was pivotal for both the individual investor and the entrepreneur. The value of options increased with the lower capital gains rate, which provided a greater incentive for investors and entrepreneurs to accept risk. Historically, the government provided considerable support for small business through tax incentives, support for SBICs, and so forth. Unfortunately, this underlying philosophy of support for small business is less evident in today's political climate.

VENTURE INVESTING CYCLE

Portfolio managers considering investing in venture capital must understand the venture cycle before they can decide how venture capital fits into their asset allocation structure. The first step is to decide whether venture capital is appropriate given their portfolio objectives. The second step is to develop a strategy for investing in venture capital. A carefully constructed strategy provides the important foundation from which to evaluate potential portfolio investments. We know with great clarity where and when we *should have* invested; it is much more difficult to determine where and when one *should be* investing. A well-diversified, dollar-averaged program structured for investing over time helps both to mitigate the risk of uncertainty and to rationalize the decision process.

Diversification is a critical issue in venture investing, just as it is with equity or fixed-income investments. One can diversify by style, by approach, by geographic region (although this has become much less important than it was historically), and by the stage of financing. A particular program may even include a decision not to diversify fully. For example, either a public pension fund or a local company pension fund may believe that it is in the employees' best interest to bias the venture capital portfolio either for or against its own region. The first decision would be based on promoting the local economy; the second, to hedge against it. Such decisions would, of course, depend on the particular situation of the fund.

Finally, a caveat: beware of fads. If you have carefully thought through how you want to approach investing in venture capital, you will be protected from being trampled by the herd. Plan, be disciplined, and execute. Emotional investment decisions usually result in buying at the top and selling at the bottom.

Question and Answer Session

QUESTION: Please comment on whether pressure by investors and limited partners to produce results affects the general partner's ability to perform.

KANE: In my opinion, venture capitalists can put so much pressure on portfolio companies that they could fail. The extent to which this has occurred might be debated because you are always operating in a gray area—it often seems as though the management team never has anything to show for the amount of money invested. Then the venture capitalist is faced with a decision: Do you put in more money or do you close down the company? Venture capitalists never actually close a company, they simply withdraw funding and the company closes. A number of companies are cut off from funding too early in their cycles. Maybe if a little bit more money had been put in they would be success stories today. Other companies that continue to receive funding should have been shut down after the first round of financing.

I do not think we put enough pressure on venture capitalists, nor do we spend enough time understanding the specific portfolios or determining whether the venture capitalists are executing their stated strategy. We all have a fiduciary duty to hold the venture capitalists' feet to the fire, and not get involved in their day-to-day operations and decision-making, but to ensure that the promised strategy is being executed.

QUESTION: Please comment on how the due-diligence process, both for direct and indirect investments, relates to the management teams.

KANE: The due-diligence process for direct investments begins with the management team. The first step is to evaluate the credentials of management. Generally, one looks for red flags in an initial meeting—holes in resumes, for example. We did this with one company and found out that there was a hole between 1982 and 1983. The individual claimed that he had tried something that did not work. It turns out that the person had been under indictment; needless to say, we did not go forward with the investment. Unfortunately, a number of venture capitalists invested in the company, and it has turned out to be a colossal failure. We also have a requirement that we will not invest in a company unless 20 due-diligence calls have been made on management and written up. Some of those are provided by management; others are obtained from our own resources.

The due-diligence process for indirect investments is fairly similar. We will not invest in a partnership unless we have made and documented 20 due-diligence calls on that partnership. Most of the industry has done a good job of checking the backgrounds of the venture capitalists. Eighty percent of the due-diligence process is done through telephone calling.

QUESTION: Please elaborate on how the equity split between the founders, the management, and the investor group is determined.

KANE: Normally in an early-stage company, the founders *are* the management. It is fairly typical at this stage that the providers of capital get about half the equity in the company and the founders/management get the other half. The split is a function of how the company is doing, what is happening in the capital markets, and what the market environment for capital is at that point in time. Today, you would probably get more of a company than you would have in 1983. Even though these are early-stage, private financings, they are influenced by conditions in the public market environment—which is only natural, because that is the ultimate exit everyone is striving for. As the company progresses, the management and the initial investor group take a similar amount of dilution—the difference being that the existing investor group, particularly in today's marketplace, is generally required to put up half the amount of the next financing to get the deal done. That way, if you are getting promoted, they are promoting themselves as well. To commit that kind of capital at that price, they must really believe in the company.

QUESTION: How do you value a company in the start-up and early stage?

KANE: Generally, the company's value equals the discounted value of what the company is estimated to be worth in the future, if everything goes according to plan. Valuations might be influenced by the fact that the investment is in a capital-intensive industry, is likely to need subsequent rounds of financing, or is an early-stage company that is not capital-intensive and thus will most likely not need additional financings before it gets to cash flow break-even. The latter company would command a much higher valuation than the former. Valuations also reflect the quality of the management team, the industry in which the company is operating, the potential for that industry, and the marketplace. There is no science to it; it is a question of what the market will bear, a trial and error process.

QUESTION: What are the new areas of venture capital investment?

KANE: There are four things that venture capitalists will be doing in the future that they were not doing three or four years ago. The first area is consolidation financings. There are companies that do not have enough critical mass to cover their overhead or pay for their marketing field force. The goal is to build a big company—and these companies are never going to achieve it. One solution is to combine two companies that are in the same situation. They can share the same marketing force, office space, and administrative staff. In the future, the merger or consolidation of similar companies in similar industries will take up quite a bit of venture capitalists' time.

Second, when a venture capitalist sees a company that has $10 or $12 million in revenues and a management team that can run a $100 to $200 million company, he must decide whether to build the company to $200 million or acquire a bigger company. Interestingly, small companies are acquiring larger companies more frequently in today's marketplace.

Third, leveraged buyouts in technology areas are becoming more common. A number of technology companies could succeed with a different financial architecture, and the venture capital industry is addressing itself to this. In fact, I am rather bullish today on some of the biotechnology companies that have been around for five or six years. One could build a portfolio with restarts in biotechnology companies—ones that have tired investors, have run out of capital, or cannot grow because they cannot attract the capital. With an infusion of capital, new management, changes in market focus, and perhaps research and development and engineering, they could be viable companies again.

The fourth area is the recapitalization of public companies. There are a number of companies that should not have gone public over the past five years because they were not far enough along in the product life cycle to have staying power as a public company. These companies fall into what is referred to as the "earnings-per-share trap" where the marketplace kills them every quarter they do not produce good earnings. Some companies lose two-thirds of their value in the public marketplace because they tripped or stumbled in a calendar quarter, even though it might be for perfectly justifiable reasons. So the recapitalization of public companies by venture capitalists will still generally be privately placed stock of public companies. Frequently, the stock will be sold at a discount off the public market price—sometimes at discounts of 30 to 50 percent. Normally, it will be a preferred issue; the existing public investors will hold common stock and the venture capitalists will hold the preferred shares. In the event that things do not work out or the company has to be merged, the venture capitalists will come out first. The recapitalization of public companies—frequently turnaround candidates—will be taking a lot of time in the venture capital industry, and may represent a very attractive investment opportunity.

QUESTION: What are your return-on-investment expectations for venture capital by stage of investment in the 1990s?

KANE: Obviously, an early-stage investor needs a significantly higher potential return to justify making the investment. For a start-up round of financing, the rate of return should exceed 35 percent, because the casualty rate of start-up companies is very high. In the expansion rounds, the rate of return should be in excess of 20 percent. I do not think one should ever do a financing where the rate of return expectations are less than 20 percent, because there will not be enough profit to cover the losers. As one gets further out in the investment stage continuum, the down side is better protected. The risk of loss can be minimized through financial techniques such as liquidation preferences, take-me-along provisions in the event of a merger, and participating preferred stock. In these cases, a rate of return in the twenties would be acceptable.

Overall, I think the opportunities in the venture capital industry are attractive. It is a very cyclical industry. Today, we are at a cyclical low for technology stocks. Things probably cannot get much worse from the point of view of the public markets. We are not likely, at least in the next 10 years, to see a frothy, euphoric market like the 1983 market. The industry has demonstrated, however, that it is possible to make very healthy returns with just a decent, acceptable public market environment like we had in March or April of 1987. That period did not represent a particularly frothy market; it was a healthy market. I have no reason to believe that returns will not be as attractive as our expectations were a number of years ago.

QUESTION: How large should a pension fund be before considering venture capital as an asset class?

CATTANACH: The minimum size of the fund seeking a venture capital investment program structured to fit its unique investment profile, needs, and objectives should be approximately $200 million. Smaller funds cannot achieve adequate diversification. Typically, the venture capital component is allocated 1 to 5 percent of the total asset base, which would be approximately $10 million at 5 percent of a $200 million fund. In my opinion, a minimum of $10 to $20 million is required to achieve adequate diversification in a venture capital partnership portfolio.

A smaller fund could participate through a fund-of-funds portfolio. This is a pooled fund concept, similar in many ways to a common fund or a mutual fund. The amount required to invest would be less; however, the drawback is that the investor cannot tailor the investment to fit his or her particular situation.

Setting Realistic Expectations for Potential Returns—Part I

T. Bondurant French, CFA

The process of setting expectations for asset returns involves analyzing historical risk and return data for all asset classes in the investable capital market, and then extrapolating into the future. In this presentation, I am going to discuss the data necessary for setting expectations for venture capital returns.

HISTORICAL RETURNS AND RISK

The process of setting realistic expectations for venture capital returns must be done within the context of all the other asset classes in the investable capital market. Table 1 shows 10-year annualized returns and standard deviations for eight asset classes and inflation, for December 1977 through December 1987. The table indicates that the compound return for venture capital was 23.2 percent over the period. The spread between venture capital and small-capitalization stock returns was 610 basis points, and the return spread between venture capital and large-capitalization stocks, in a particularly good period for large capitalization stocks, was 900 basis points. The return over inflation during this period was an enormous 1,680 basis points.

This period may be characterized as a "good" period for venture capital, but it should actually be divided into two subperiods. The first half of the period, from 1977 to 1983, was particularly good for venture capital; compound rates of return on limited partnerships were 35 to 45 percent, and sometimes higher. Returns in the period since 1983 have been flat. Therefore, one should be careful in drawing investment expectations about venture capital from historical data. The period of the late 1970s and early 1980s should not be considered a full cycle, so return expectations should be somewhat lower than the 25 percent that many people expect.

Table 2 shows the investable capital market's performance characteristics over a much longer period, from December 31, 1959, to December 31, 1987. Over this 28-year annualized period, returns to venture capital were 15.3 percent. Over this period, venture capital returned about 410 basis points more than small-capitalization stocks and 640 basis points more than large-capitalization stocks. Venture capital had a 1,030 basis-point real advantage over inflation.

While the venture capital results versus equities during this period may appear narrow, remember that these are 28-year compound returns. The investment of $1.00 at a 15.3 percent compound rate of return over 28 years becomes $53.85. One dollar invested at the small capitalization stock return of 11.2 percent becomes $19.54 over the same period.

SOURCES OF VENTURE CAPITAL DATA

The venture capital data comprise a combination of data series. Since 1983, the data are based on the results of the partnerships in which First Chicago participated (with a 70 percent weighting) and the results of the Wilshire $10-$100 million market capitalization index (with a 30 percent weighting). From 1959 to 1983, the data are a composite of the publicly traded venture capital companies—not the companies backed by venture capitalists, but the venture capital companies in corporate rather than partnership form. Approximately 25 or 30 of these companies were formed in the 1960s. Because of the changing tax laws and low stock prices, most of these companies were liquidated, and only about five remain in existence today. Consequently, these data do not measure many of the very successful private partnerships that were formed, so the returns shown may be low; nor do the data measure some of the partnerships that were formed and did poorly. We believe our long-term return number of 15.3 percent is probably about right as an historical measure.

EXPECTED RETURNS AND RISK

For each of these asset classes, Table 3 shows what the long-term equilibrium return, expected return, and risk are expected to be over the next five years.

TABLE 1.	Investable Capital Market Performance Characteristics (12/31/77-12/31/87)

	Annualized Return	Standard Deviation[1]
Venture Capital	23.2%	23.1%
International Equity	21.7	17.6
Small-Capitalization Equity	17.1	21.9
Non-Dollar Bonds	14.3	14.2
Large-Capitalization Equity	14.2	16.7
Real Estate	12.6	2.8
Domestic Fixed-Income	10.4	10.0
T-Bills	9.2	1.3
Inflation	*6.4*	*2.1*

[1]Calculated using quarterly logarithmic returns and then annualized.

Source: First Chicago Investment Advisors

TABLE 2.	Investable Capital Market Performance Characteristics (12/31/59-12/31/87)

	Annualized Return	Standard Deviation[1]
Venture Capital	15.3%	35.8%
International Equity	12.6	16.5
Small-Capitalization Equity	11.2	22.9
Non-Dollar Bonds	9.3	12.2
Large-Capitalization Equity	8.9	16.6
Real Estate	8.5	2.4
Domestic Fixed-Income	6.5	8.2
T-Bills	6.3	1.4
Inflation	*5.0*	*1.8*

[1]Calculated using quarterly logarithmic returns and then annualized.

Source: First Chicago Investment Advisors

Note that venture capital has the highest equilibrium and expected return: 18.5 percent for an equilibrium return and 17.0 percent for an expected return. The difference between the two is pretty much noise for venture capital, so there is no reason to be underweighted or overweighted in the asset class based on these numbers. For some of the other asset classes, for example dollar bonds or U.S. equities, the percentage points have more significance. We are assuming 5 percent inflation in these forecasts. The 45 percent standard deviation attached to venture capital is really a "fudged" number. We have never experienced volatility that high, but it is important to include something in the risk measure that captures the significant illiquidity risk in the venture capital business. The 17 percent expected return for venture capital is lower than has been experienced in the past 10 years, but it seems to be in line with the long-term results, and would be a very satisfying future long-term return versus other asset classes.

Table 4 presents long-term asset-class equilibrium return correlation forecasts. The standard deviation of venture capital alone is very high, at 45 percent. The venture capital asset class is not highly correlated with the other asset classes, however. Therefore, when venture capital is added to a portfolio, it does not add much incremental risk. The data indicate that venture capital returns are not highly correlated with inflation over long time periods; therefore, there is no positive correlation between venture capital results and that of real estate, nor any negative correlation with bonds. Venture capital results have not been highly correlated with movements in currencies either, nor have they been highly correlated with movements in the general economy and, therefore, movements in large-capitalization stocks. Venture capital results have been most highly correlated with movements in small-capitalization stocks, but still not to the same degree that a small-capitalization stock is to the equity market.

The result of this analysis is that even with return expectations of 18 to 20 percent, venture capital is an attractive asset class for investors. It is an excellent diversifier and can improve the total portfolio's risk-return profile.

Where are we today in terms of returns? Table 5 shows the average cumulative internal rate of return (IRR) to the limited partner for a series of venture capital funds. This table includes all the data for our 74 partnerships, plus a survey of partnership data

TABLE 3. Long-Term Asset Class Equilibrium and Expected Returns (9/30/88)

Asset Class	Equilibrium Return	Expected Return[1]	Risk
U.S. Equity	12.0%	11.2%	17.5%
Non-U.S. Equity	11.8	6.9	19.5
Venture Capital	18.5	17.0	45.0
Dollar Bonds	8.1	9.9	7.5
Non-Dollar Bonds	8.2	6.6	9.0
Real Estate	10.2	8.0	14.0
Cash Equivalents	6.4	6.7	1.5
Multiple Markets Index	11.1%	9.9%	11.9%

[1]Annualized five-year return; assumes 5 percent inflation.

Source: First Chicago Investment Advisors

TABLE 4. Long-Term Asset Class Equilibrium Returns Correlation Forecasts[1]

	1	2	3	4	5	6	7
1. U.S. Equity	1.00						
2. Non-U.S. Equity	0.60	1.00					
3. Venture Capital	0.35	0.15	1.00				
4. Dollar Bonds	0.45	0.25	0.15	1.00			
5. Non-Dollar Bonds	0.25	0.60	0.10	0.30	1.00		
6. Real Estate	0.35	0.30	0.25	0.20	0.15	1.00	
7. Cash Equivalents	-0.10	-0.15	-0.10	-0.05	-0.10	0.25	1.00

[1] Annualized returns

Source: First Chicago Investment Advisors

from other limited partners. These data show that partnerships formed in 1979 had a one-year return of 18 percent; partnerships formed in 1979 had a two-year compound return in 1980 of 26 percent; and so on. The older partnerships have had a chance to mature; the companies in their portfolios have had a chance to grow so that they are interesting enough to be acquired or to go public. The resulting returns are evident. The younger partnerships are showing poorer returns. It takes three or four years for most venture capitalists to find investments, so it is meaningless to look at results for very short time periods. In addition, the "lemons" seem to ripen early, so there is a stronger potential for negative results in the early years, with the more positive results taking place in later years. These data also reflect a certain amount of cyclicality. Because of the high valuations in the 1982 and 1983 period, funds formed in that period are probably going to be a disappointment, achieving results of less than 20 percent. Funds formed since 1984 are getting better results, particularly in terms of the quality of the companies in their portfolio.

It is important to report performance statistics for the venture capital industry in a useful format. A good reporting format lists the partnerships in chronological order to illustrate the performance of the older partnerships relative to the newer funds. We calculate the returns of our partnerships on a quarterly basis. On an interim basis, we are not as concerned with the number itself as the change in the number from quarter to quarter. This type of report is a good exceptions report. If a particular IRR jumps up or down compared to the previous quarter, something significant is happening in that partnership and attention should be focused on it.

In summary, we believe that venture capital is an excellent diversifier for a plan sponsor's portfolio, improving the portfolio return without adding significant incremental risk. Venture capital results should continue to provide above-average returns in the future—comparable to those achieved over the past several decades, but not equivalent to the spectacular results of the late 1970s and early 1980s.

TABLE 5. Average Cumulative IRR to the Limited Partner For Venture Capital Funds

Year of Fund Formation	1979	1980	1981	1982	1983	1984	1985	1986	1987
1979	18%	26%	35%	30%	40%	29%	28%	26%	23%
1980	-	2	10	23	34	26	20	20	20
1981	-	-	2	2	20	10	11	8	9
1982	-	-	-	0	17	5	3	2	6
1983	-	-	-	-	0	7	4	5	5
1984	-	-	-	-	-	2	-2	-1	3
1985	-	-	-	-	-	-	3	3	7
1986	-	-	-	-	-	-	-	-1	1

(Year of Calculation across columns 1979–1987)

Source: First Chicago Investment Advisors

Setting Realistic Expectations for Potential Returns—Part II

Linda A. Vincent

In this presentation, I will discuss the process of setting realistic expectations for potential returns in venture capital investing. Many people use the terms "performance" and "returns" interchangeably; this is inappropriate. In the early years of a venture capital partnership, the book value of the partnership simply does not reflect any equivalent of a fair market value. There are only unrealizable valuations to rely on.

INDUSTRY GROWTH AND PERFORMANCE

A major factor that complicates setting performance expectations is the size and recent growth of the industry. The industry's small size is a real plus to investors who seek diversification in smaller, less efficient markets. In fact, the entire industry is smaller than some of the largest U.S. pension funds. To get some perspective on the size of this industry, in seven of the past eight years, IBM's research and development expenditures were higher than the amount that the venture capital industry invested in small business development. The recent growth of the industry has caused other problems. Over half of all private, independent venture firms operating today were formed in the 1980s, and one-quarter of the entire universe has been formed since the end of 1984—that means that 25 percent of the industry has come into being in the past three years. In the 10-year time span from 1978 to 1987, the amount of capital under management has grown tenfold. On a constant dollar basis, it is still an increase of six times the amount of money that was under management 10 years ago.

The sudden growth has created some problems regarding performance evaluation. The problems confronting investors in venture capital are: (1) How does one assess a short track record? (2) How does one assess a management team that has not been through a complete venture capital cycle? and (3) What are reasonable future expectations for the asset class?

One obvious reason to invest in venture capital is to participate in the opportunity for higher overall returns, by diversifying into fragmented or less efficient market sectors. Figure 1 shows the returns to several asset classes over a 20-year period, using data based on the results of a Venture Economics study first published over six years ago. On a long-term basis, venture capital outperformed all other asset classes. Nevertheless, in the short run, any one of these categories can outperform venture capital.

Because data on venture capital partnerships are not available, many people use as a proxy the Venture Capital 100, which is an index of publicly traded, venture-backed companies. Figure 2 shows how the Venture Capital 100 Index has performed relative to three stock indexes: the Value Line Composite, the Standard & Poor's 500, and the NASDAQ. Over the past 15 years, a dollar invested in these venture-backed companies (now public) would have far outperformed the broad market indexes, but not without volatility.

The performance of a venture capital fund depends on the performance of the underlying portfolio companies. Several years ago, we did a study of returns to venture funds. The study looked at 13 funds organized by 10 management groups. This study was limited to groups that had completed their investment cycles, having fully liquidated all the underlying investments. In other words, there was no speculation in the numbers. Figure 3 shows the distribution of returns to a typical venture fund based on the results of this study. In this group, nearly two-thirds of the investments either lost money or were barely above break-even. Over 15 percent of the investments returned five or more times the invested capital. How long did they have to wait for these results? Only 31 percent of these investments were held less than three years. Roughly half of the investments were held five years or longer. And finally, over 40 percent of the complete losers appeared in the first 2.5 years of the funds' investment cycles. The majority of significant winners were held five years or more.

FIGURE 1. Average Annual Rates of Return Over 20 Years or Greater Period

Percent

Short-Term Investments	3.7
U.S. Common Stocks	10.1
Emerging Growth Stocks	15.3
Bonds	4.5
Foreign Common Stock	10.9
Real Estate	7.7
Gold	6.0
Venture Capital	27.1

Source: Venture Economics

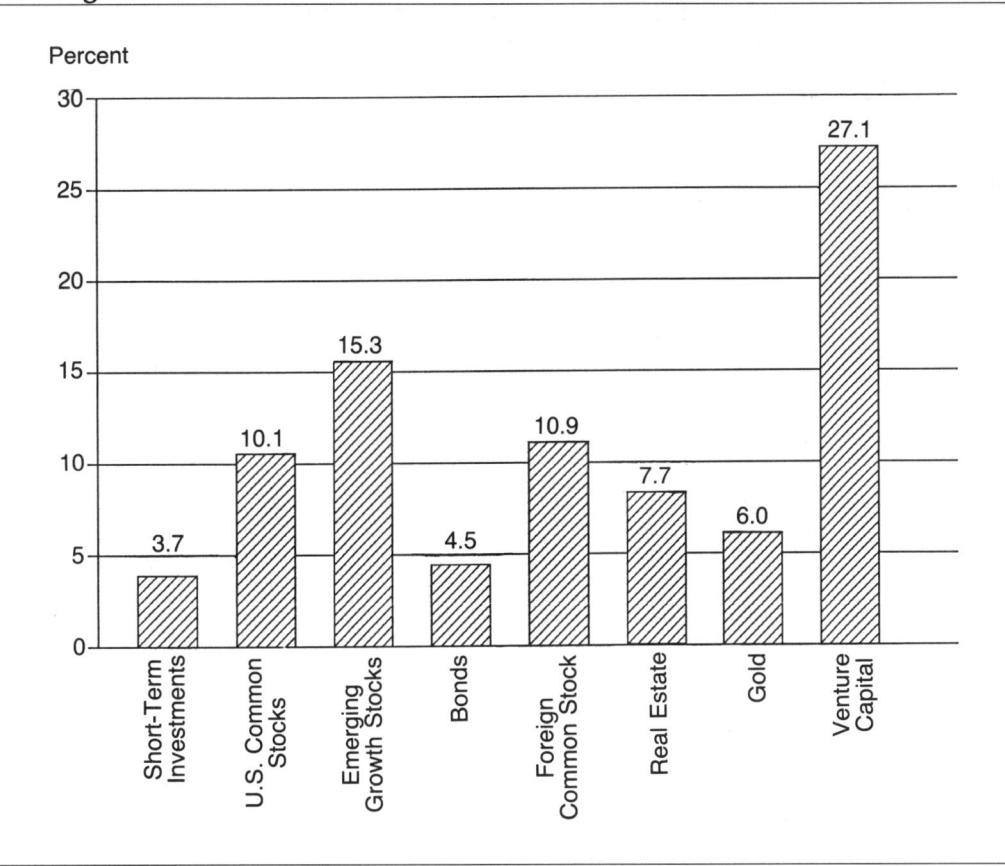

FIGURE 2. Quarterly Index

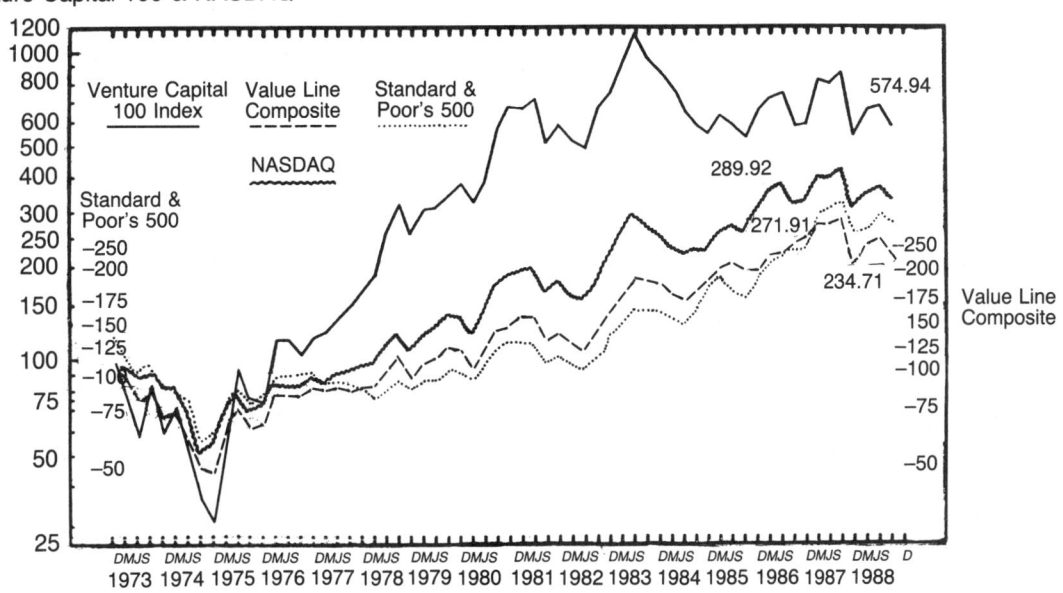

Venture Capital 100 & NASDAQ

Values at end: Venture Capital 100 Index 289.92; Standard & Poor's 500 574.94 (right scale); NASDAQ 271.91; Value Line Composite 234.71.

X-axis: DMJS quarterly ticks, 1973–1988.

Source: Venture Economics

FIGURE 3. The Distribution of Returns to a Typical Venture Fund

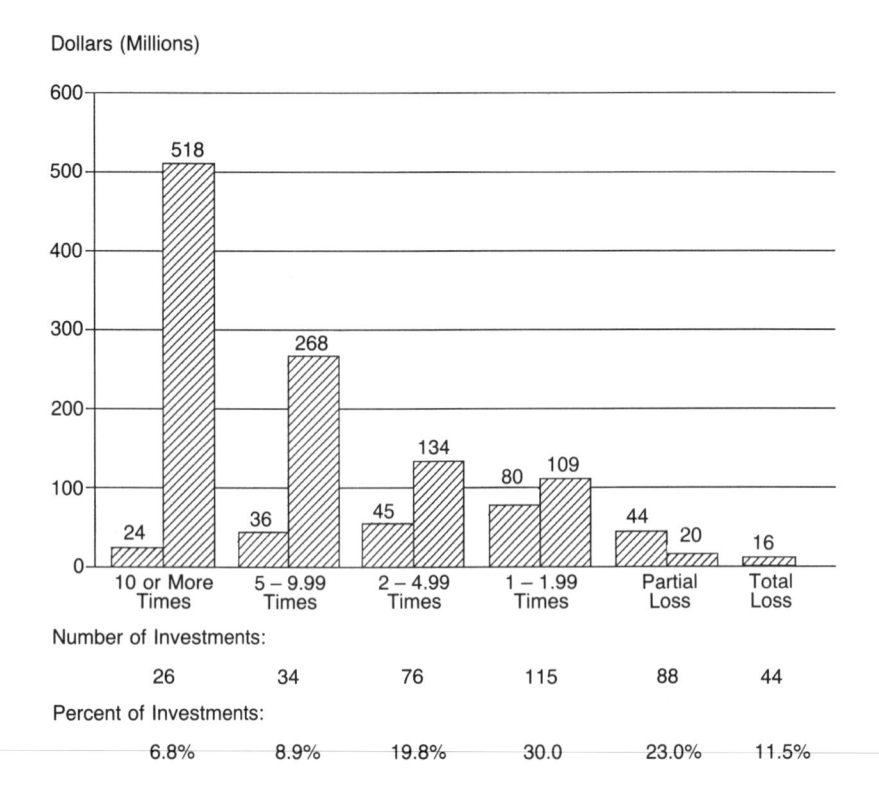

Dollars (Millions)

	10 or More Times	5 – 9.99 Times	2 – 4.99 Times	1 – 1.99 Times	Partial Loss	Total Loss
	24 / 518	36 / 268	45 / 134	80 / 109	44 / 20	16 / —
Number of Investments:	26	34	76	115	88	44
Percent of Investments:	6.8%	8.9%	19.8%	30.0	23.0%	11.5%

Source: Venture Economics

PATTERNS OF RETURNS TO VENTURE CAPITAL

The pattern of returns in the venture capital industry affects performance. Table 1 shows a model of a cash flow program in a typical fund. Limited partner contributions are made in the front end. In this example, contributions are made in three tranches over a 24-month period. That is no longer typical—the take-down period is being stretched out; a number of venture funds are calling capital as needed, more like a leveraged buyout (LBO) model. The bottom row is the reported net asset value of the capital account at the end of the 12-month period. The model treats the remaining portfolio net asset value as through it were converted to cash. In this example, it is not until years six, seven, eight, or nine that one begins to get significant payouts. By year 10, the capital account value is down to a very small amount. The return on this fund is good: a six-times payout on $1.5 million invested, which is roughly $9 million returned over the 10-year period.

Any discussion of patterns of returns must highlight the causes of these patterns and the most influential factors. Performance calculations are most strongly affected by the take-down schedule, the valuations of the underlying portfolio companies, and the timing and recognition of distributions. In the early years, valuations include realized and perhaps unrealizable appreciation, as well as unrealized losses. Because there are no standards in our industry, different benchmarks are used to value companies such as public market multiples. Nevertheless, there are a number of venture partnerships that have invested in the same syndicated round of a particular company, but are not holding it at the same value.

Another factor is the timing and recognition of distributions. Several issues affect distributions. For example, will the general partners begin to deduct their carried interest investment by investment? Or, will they wait to deduct their carried interest until after they have paid back the limited partners all of their contributed capital? The way in which management fees are handled is another issue. Typically, fees are deducted from the partners' capital accounts, but they may be billed separately.

Table 2 shows the median internal rates of return (IRR) in 1987 for a sample of 150 funds by fund age. Overall, the analysis shows that the period of the

TABLE 1. Cash Flow Model: Venture Capital Partnership

	\multicolumn{10}{c}{As of Year:}
	1	2	3	4	5	6	7	8	9	10
Contribution	500	500	500	—	—	—	—	—	—	—
Distribution	—	—	100	100	300	800	1,800	2,000	3,000	900
Capital Account Value	490	850	1,100	1,500	2,500	3,600	4,000	4,000	1,000	< 100

Source: Venture Economics

early to mid-1980s is not developing at the same rate or to the same levels as the period of the late 1970s.

The 1970s are broken down into two groups: funds formed in the early 1970s and funds formed in the late 1970s. The first group of funds (1970-76) has completed a full investment cycle. These funds had a median internal rate of return of 20 percent in their tenth year. The range was from about 13 percent to 30 percent, with an average of a little over 21 percent. The funds in this group followed the traditional J-curve pattern; they had returned all of the limited partners' contributed capital and were profitable by year seven.

Funds in the second group were formed in the late 1970s (1977-79). The median rate of return for this group was over 25 percent; the average was 33 percent. This group had uncharacteristically high performance in the early years—a pattern not seen before. The (1977-79) funds had returned all contributed capital and were profitable by year four—a significant difference.

The funds formed in the 1980s have not completed the full investment cycle. For funds that were formed between 1980 and 1982, we saw skyrocketing internal rates of return, peaking in 1983, and then dramatic declines until 1985, then two years of stabilization. For the funds formed in 1980, the median IRR is just over 15 percent, and the average internal rate of return is just over 19 percent. At the upper level of the range, we have an outlier returning over 52 percent, compounded. For the 1981 funds, the median return is just over 5 percent, and the average about 9 percent. These funds had returned three-quarters of the capital contributed by the end of year six. For the 1982 funds, it appears as though our sample has fallen out of bed—the median internal rate of return is 1 percent, and the average is just below zero. The amount distributed by these funds at the end of their fifth year of life—as of December 31, 1987—was much less than funds of that age that were formed in previous years.

Funds formed since 1983 have not operated in the same atmosphere of volatility. Our 1983 sample has a median return just below 3 percent and an average just below 4 percent. Less than 20 percent of the paid-in capital has been returned, so these numbers are really based on unrealized appreciation and depreciation.

TABLE 2. Median Internal Rates of Return by Fund Age

Year of Fund Formation	1	2	3	4	5	As of Year: 6	7	8	9	10
1970 to 1976	9.0%	8.8%	2.4%	5.4%	7.5%	14.3%	20.5%	19.2%	17.9%	20.0%
1977 to 1979	6.3	27.8	28.5	30.7	35.1	28.8	27.3	26.4	35.1*	
1980	2.9	13.8	35.2	24.7	21.8	17.1	15.1			
1981	5.8	25.6	12.4	5.5	5.6	5.1				
1982	14.8	4.6	-2.9	-0.5	1.0					
1983	0.7	0.0	1.3	2.7						
1984	-1.2	-1.2	1.6							
1985	0.4	1.1								
1986	-1.7									

* The year 9 data is only for funds formed 1977 to 1978.

Source: Venture Economics

The final cohort, 1984 funds, has a median return of 1.6 percent and an average of 0.5 percent. Less than 10 percent of the paid-in capital has been returned.

UNDERSTANDING THE DATA

It is important to understand the characteristics of this sample and how they might differ from other data. One-third of our sample consists of early-stage focused funds, and that alone can explain some of the performance data. Also, the majority of the funds in this sample are first-time funds. Most experienced investors and advisors establish their venture capital portfolio by selecting the venture groups that have the longest track record and individuals that have worked together as a team before. The differences in samples will make a big difference in venture capital performance.

It is very important to keep in mind that there is tremendous diversity in the venture industry now that was not there 10 years ago. This diversity will affect the performance statistics and how well one looks relative to historical performance statistics. It would be a great mistake to compare these very different investment strategy styles within the same cohort group.

Some of the real thorny issues involving performance measurement have to do with the fact that this is a very young industry. First, for all intents and purposes, we have only 20 years of meaningful data, and in the first 10 of those 20 years, the universe is so small that yearly comparisons would be invalid. Second, there are a lot of venture firms that do not manage institutional money. We track data on over 650 venture firms, but less than 250 of those firms manage institutional money. Finally, there is a structural difficulty in the industry: the number of observations per year is inadequate. Ideally, to be statistically rigorous, the database should consist of weekly or monthly observations, but most of the funds issue unaudited quarterly financial reports; some only provide semi-annual reports and some others only provide annual reports. There is only one audited annual report for any of these funds, but the auditors state that they cannot confirm the underlying values of these investments.

EXPECTATIONS FOR THE FUTURE

To obtain a forecast of future returns to venture capital, we polled limited partners and investment advisors on their expectations for the future. Their outlook, surprisingly, was almost unanimous: Returns will be in the high teens. Had this same group been polled seven or eight years ago, the outlook would most likely have been for returns in the 20 to 25 percent range compounded, compared to returns in the 15 to 20 percent range now. If venture capital partnership returns fall much below that, investors are going to take a long hard look at other areas of investment. Venture must earn a premium over risk-free investments to make up for its lack of liquidity.

Finally, the challenge for limited partners who are investing in venture capital partnerships is to make the venture capitalists accountable. Attend the meetings, ask the questions, pay attention to what is in the portfolio. But also allow them to manage for the long term.

Question and Answer Session

QUESTION: Please comment on the different valuation techniques that venture capital companies use. Are these techniques comparable?

FRENCH: We have been pleasantly surprised by the consistency of the valuation techniques used by venture capitalists in analyzing their companies. It is very difficult to evaluate these small, rapidly growing, privately held companies. There seem to be very few problem situations, however. The exceptions are primarily caused by timing problems. Investors who have a large enough sample should not be particularly concerned about different valuation methods.

The timing differences seem to be most evident during fundraising. Our data include a broad array of funds, with 74 partnerships, 5 international funds, and 69 domestic funds of varying ages. There are seed funds, growth-stage funds, later-stage funds, and focused funds.

VINCENT: My principal concern is with the manipulation of numbers just prior to marketing a new fund. I think some of the pressure to show strong numbers comes from the limited partners who want to know how a fund has done. As a result, there is increasing pressure to perform, not just on paper, but also in reality. We feel that our principal role is to highlight the red flags and to let the investors do their own due diligence.

QUESTION: Do you calculate statistics for industry- or stage-type relative performance?

VINCENT: Yes, but there are not enough data to make the statistics meaningful yet. Industry-focused venture funds are still relatively new, so we do not have 10-year track records on any of these managers. For example, we are calculating statistics on one sample that is 2.5 years into what will be 12- to 14-year investment programs, so it is simply a matter of time before meaningful conclusions can be drawn. One way to make the subset large enough is to compare focused groups that were formed in different calendar years, but we hesitate to do that until we become comfortable with the available baseline data. It would be incorrect to compare seed funds and late-stage funds three years into their respective investment programs because of the difference in investment style.

FRENCH: We have done some regression analysis on venture capital data to try to build a model that would help us pick better partnerships.

The data showed, at least historically, that the partnerships that have performed the best were the ones that had a single office, had experienced partners, were national in scope, and were opportunistic with respect to the industry. Funds that put constraints on the opportunities being considered, either territorially or industry-wise, had weaker performance. For the future, in a more competitive environment, perhaps focused funds will do better. Right now, we just do not know.

QUESTION: What will commitment levels be in the next few years?

VINCENT: Most of the very large, new investors appear to use a basket approach. Many of these investors categorize investments in leveraged buyout funds in that same basket. I think there has been a shift in fund allocations out of venture and into LBOs; this will result in some contraction in terms of dollars coming into the venture industry. Some funds and fund-management groups will go out of business; people are human, they make mistakes, and they fail. This contraction will have an impact on relative returns and the industry's ability to attract capital.

FRENCH: The pace of pension fund commitment to venture capital will probably stay relatively constant. The performance of the partnerships that people already have backed will influence commitment levels. A number of clients who have been involved in venture capital since 1983 may be disillusioned with the results they have gotten so far; they have waited almost six years, and their committees are starting to run out of patience. Some of these clients may reduce additional commitments to venture capital. On the other hand, there are a number of players who are willing to invest throughout the cycle. These people understand the venture capital process and are willing to invest now despite the bleak outlook. Yet, most money was made in venture capital in the late 1970s and early 1980s, by people who invested in the mid-1970s when the future looked quite bleak. I have been surprised at how consistent some of the pension funds have been in terms of their annual allocations and commitments.

Valuing Potential Investments—Part I

C. Kevin Landry

There are many strategies for valuing potential investments in the venture capital markets. I will outline the key considerations, using my experience at TA Associates as an example.

Potential venture capital investments must meet the investment criteria and fit the portfolio strategy of the individual investors. In our firm, the investment criteria are fairly straightforward. First, we are looking for complete and proven management teams. Often, we will find companies that do not have such a management team in place. In these cases, we might lend them money while they do the necessary recruiting, but the full investment is not closed until the complete management team is in place.

Second, the investment must be in a market that is large and growing at a minimum of 20 percent a year. The market must have at least $100 million in sales annually in the United States and twice that if international is included. Good management and a rapidly growing market are both crucial to a successful venture investment.

Third, the number of competitors in a given market must be limited. That usually means a technological product. We also look for companies that have above-average margins. Essentially, these companies are self-financing, and it is not necessary to put more money into the company to finance its growth.

Finally, we look for an exit. We are in the business of realizing a capital gain, so we try to find a way out of an investment before we go in.

IDENTIFYING ATTRACTIVE INVESTMENTS

Identifying attractive venture capital investments is key to one's success in the venture capital market. It is important to know the characteristics of success. Table 1 shows the characteristics of some of our past investments. The investments are ranked according to various characteristics, including the management capability of the president, the quality and cohesiveness of the management team, and market size. In the biggest winners—where we made over 10 times our money—the presidents were frequently people of great vision, but were mediocre at best in managing the businesses on a day-to-day basis. What made the company successful was that they caught the market just right: their market timing was perfect, the market growth was fantastic, and the rest was easy. It is interesting that for the big winners (more than 10 times), neither the board of directors nor the president made a significant contribution to the success of the company. They were simply in the right market at the right time.

For the moderate (5 to 10 times) winners, management was the key ingredient. Those companies tended to be very well managed. The losers, for the most part, are characterized by poor timing; the markets were sizable but the growth was over. One of the worst investments, a company in the video game business called Imagic, went from zero to $82 million in revenues in its first year—and back to zero in its second year.

The venture capitalist can make the greatest contribution in the moderate-winner companies. In the really tough situations where the market has passed you by, there is not much anyone can do to salvage an investment.

The stage of a company's development is a measure of describing investment risk. In fact, the stage of development is more important in describing the risk than the round of investment. The success of investments in start-up companies is subject to the whims of the capital markets, because these companies have to raise money frequently, and if market conditions are unfavorable, severe dilution can occur. On the other hand, later-stage companies are subject to the whims of the new issue window. These risks must be accounted for in the evaluation of a company.

Contrary to conventional risk-return expectations, our highest rates of return were earned on investments in profitable companies, not start-up companies. The second highest rates of return were earned on investments in start-up companies. Stage-two companies, or development-stage companies, achieved the third highest rate of return, much lower than the first two categories. Revenue-stage companies—companies which are shipping product but not yet profitable—had marginal returns.

TABLE 1. Factors Affecting Venture Success

	Big Winners >10X	Medium Winners 5X - 10X	Losers
President	3.5	4.5	3.0
Management Team	4.0	4.25	2.75
Market Size	4.5	3.75	3.0
Market Growth	4.5	3.75	2.5
Market Timing	4.5	4.5	1.5
Margins	4.0	4.25	2.0
Proprietariness	4.0	4.0	2.25
Investment Price	4.25	3.75	3.5
Selling Price	4.5	4.0	N/A
Board of Directors	1.5	2.5	1.5

Note: Scale is 1 to 5; Worst = 1 and Best = 5.

Source: TA Associates

Figure 1 shows one view of the intrinsic value of a company over time. Obviously, it is desirable to invest where the value is rising fastest because that gives you the greatest return on investment. Based on this figure, most firms will prefer investments in the middle tier.

Our strategy is different. We believe there is too much money available for second and third stage investments, so we prefer to invest in one end of the spectrum or the other. We believe the real pricing curve is different from the traditional view illustrated in Figure 1. Figure 2 shows our view. If you get in on a start-up basis, you pay a low price but you take a lot of risk—and you get compensated for that risk. In the development and revenue stage, investors still do not know whether companies have the ingredients for success—the company's ultimate market share, how efficient their marketing organization is going to be, or their ultimate margins. So, development-and revenue-stage companies have many of the same risks as start-ups, so why a much higher price?

At the other end of the spectrum, we try to invest in profitable companies that have not been backed by other venture capitalists. In these cases, we can be the first institutional investor and essentially create a discontinuity in that curve, or create a more imperfect market by chasing companies that have not been backed by other venture capitalists.

The objective of our invested portfolio is to achieve a 30 percent compounded return on investment (ROI). Because some of that capital is not invested, however, our actual return on total capital is about 25 percent. Table 2 shows our actual performance from 1969 to the present. As is evident from the figure, it is easy to make money in a great period like the late 1970s and very difficult in tough periods like the early 1980s.

The projected performance of an investment is not evaluated using ROI. Instead, we measure how many multiples we can make on our money and over what period of time (See Table 3). We try to make 10 times our money in a start-up firm over a period of five to seven years. That works out to a 47 percent

FIGURE 1. Venture Pricing: Traditional Curve

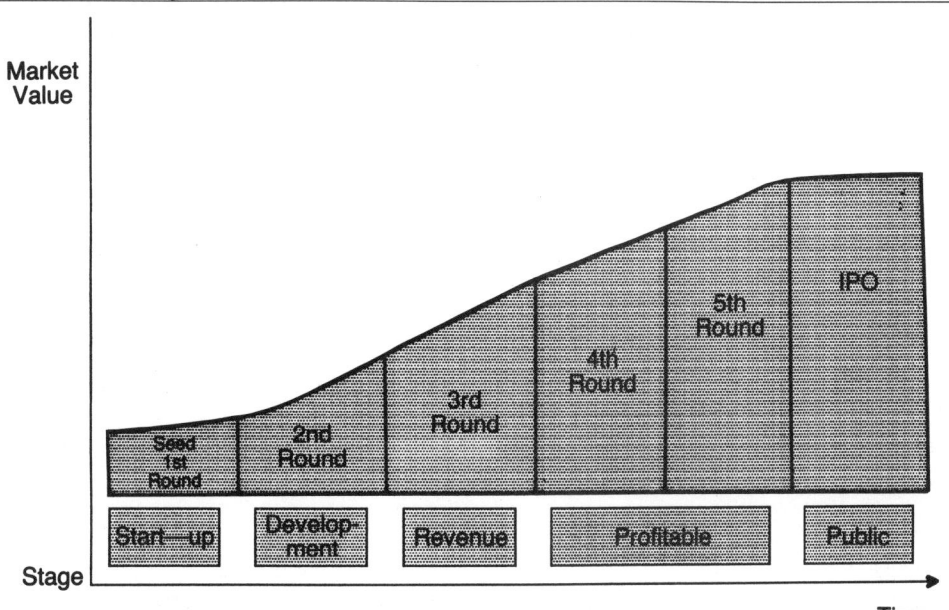

Source: TA Associates

FIGURE 2. Venture Pricing: TA Associates Curve

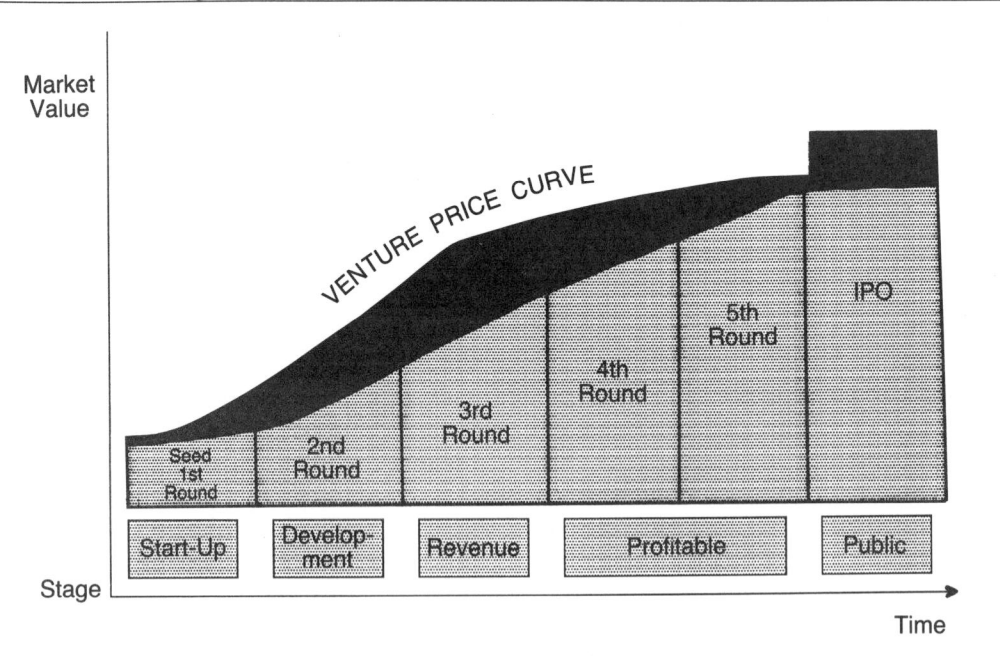

Source: TA Associates

return, compounded, on the successful investments. On development- or revenue-stage companies, we try to make four to eight times our money over an average of five years; that is a 42 percent return, compounded. On profitable companies, we try to earn three to five times our money, but over a much shorter time horizon—three years—which works out to a 37 percent return, compounded.

Rates of return on venture capital investments are extremely sensitive to time. A lot of time is spent thinking about the liquidity of investments and about how to get out of them—actually working with the companies to find merger partners or pushing them into an IPO. Table 4 shows what happens to ROI over different time periods for a given multiple on an investment. If you can make three times your money in three years, that is a 44 percent ROI. Two years later, if you can earn five times your money, the ROI is only 38 percent. So it is very important to turn over the money and realize the gains.

The risk-return profile of a potential investment depends on its stage in the life cycle. Figure 3 illustrates the differences. In the start-up category, the loss ratio is 50 percent, and the losses tend to come early. Successful investments are assumed to return 10 times an investment in seven years. An investment of $1 in each of four start-up companies would return $20 on the $4 invested, which works out to a 30 percent ROI. The opportunities for great returns in the venture business have changed. While it is still possible to make 10 times on your money, the huge home runs of 30 to 40 times on your money are not available because of competition, slower growth in the markets, or higher burn rates.

The middle-stage companies have a lower failure rate (See Figure 4). Out of four investments, we assume one failure, one mediocre investment that returns two times an investment, and two that

TABLE 2. Investment Performance

3-Year Averages

1969-71	14.75%
1972-74	22.92
1975-77	44.74
1978-80	56.16
1981-83	10.21
1984-86	25.30

Note: Return on invested portfolio by year of initial investment (valued as of 9/30/88)

Source: TA Associates

TABLE 3. Expected Returns on Individual Investments

Type	Multiple	Time	ROI
Start-Ups	10X	5-7 Years	47%
Development Stage	4-8X	4-6 Years	42%
Profitable Stage	3-5X	2-5 Years	37%

Source: TA Associates

TABLE 4. Internal Rate of Return on a Multiple of Original Investment Realized Over an Assumed Time Period

			Multiple		
Years	2	3	4	5	6
2	41	73	100	124	145
3	26	44	59	71	82
4	19	32	41	50	57
5	15	25	32	38	43
6	12	20	26	31	35

Source: TA Associates

perform well. A $4 investment in these companies would earn $14 on average; that is about a 30 percent ROI.

The loss rate is lowest for the profitable companies (See Figure 5). We assume that one out of eight investments is a loss; this also works out to an ROI of about 30 percent. Although each of these categories has the same expected ROI, the return in absolute dollar profits is quite different because of the longer holding period for start-ups.

The venture industry has lost money on about 33 percent of its investments in the 10 years ending in 1984 (Figure 6). Table 5 shows losses on 25 percent of the investments. This statistic includes both total losses and partial losses; total losses were only 11 percent. This table indicates that failures are not the issue in determining rates of return in the venture business. One must realize, however, that there are not as many opportunities to earn 20 to 30 times your money today; only a few investments get as high as 10 times.

FINDING SUCCESFUL INVESTMENTS

The process of finding investments is critical to a successful venture program. We look for rapidly growing new markets of $100 million or larger and a growth rate of 20 percent or more. Over the long term, the return on an investment will reflect the growth rate of the underlying industry. Therefore, returns in the venture business will likely outperform the ratios available on the New York Stock Exchange (NYSE), because most venture investments are in industries that are growing faster than the growth of the industries represented on the

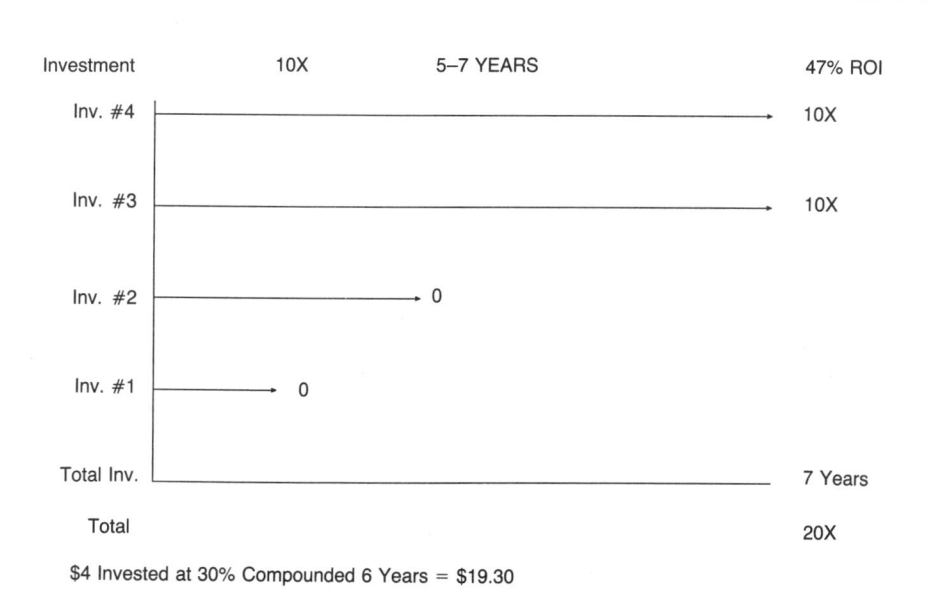

FIGURE 3. Risk-Return Profile: Startups

Investment	10X	5–7 YEARS	47% ROI
Inv. #4		→	10X
Inv. #3		→	10X
Inv. #2	→ 0		
Inv. #1	→ 0		
Total Inv.			7 Years
Total			20X

$4 Invested at 30% Compounded 6 Years = $19.30

Source: TA Associates

FIGURE 4. Risk-Return Profile: Development/Revenue Stage

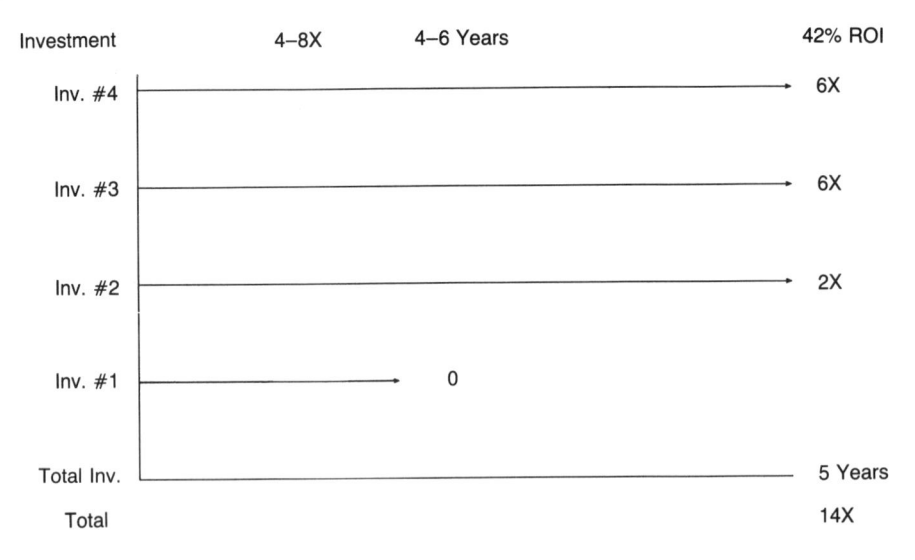

Investment	4–8X	4–6 Years	42% ROI
Inv. #4			6X
Inv. #3			6X
Inv. #2			2X
Inv. #1	0		
Total Inv.			5 Years
Total			14X

$4 Invested at 30% Compounded 5 Years = $14.80

Source: TA Associates

FIGURE 5. Risk-Return Profile: Profitable Stage

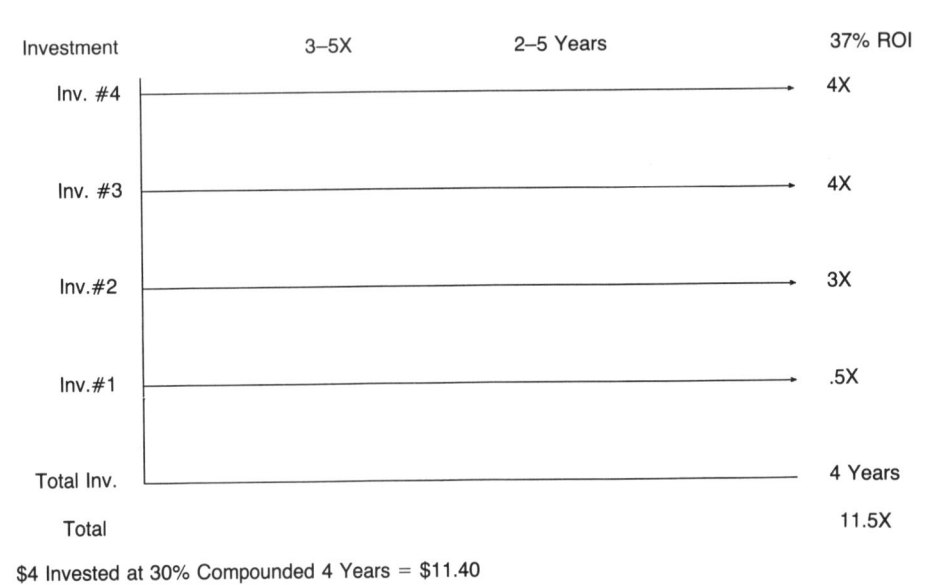

Investment	3–5X	2–5 Years	37% ROI
Inv. #4			4X
Inv. #3			4X
Inv. #2			3X
Inv. #1			.5X
Total Inv.			4 Years
Total			11.5X

$4 Invested at 30% Compounded 4 Years = $11.40

Source: TA Associates

FIGURE 6. Percent of Investments

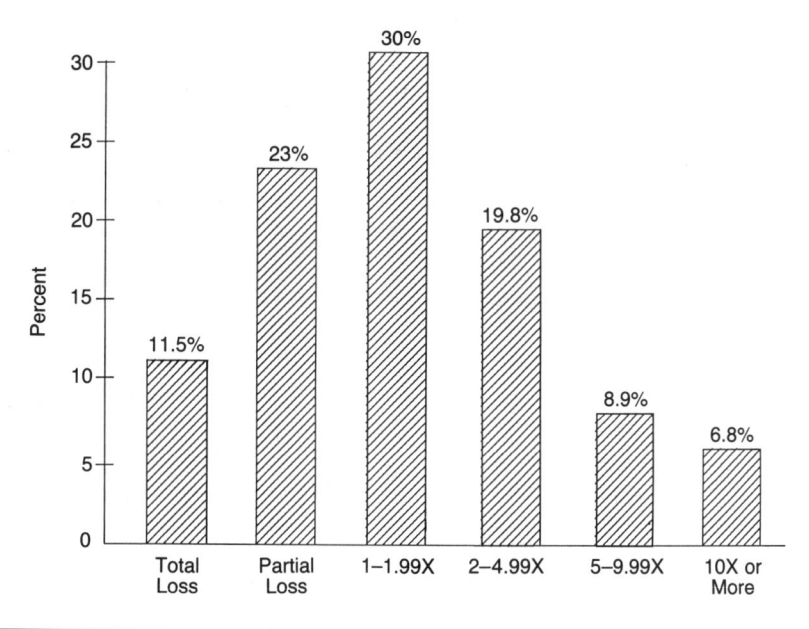

Category	Percent
Total Loss	11.5%
Partial Loss	23%
1–1.99X	30%
2–4.99X	19.8%
5–9.99X	8.9%
10X or More	6.8%

Source: Venture Economics

NYSE.

There are several industries that are attractive to venture capitalists. We are focusing on the data communications and telecommunications industries now. There will not be as many opportunities in those industries, however, as there were five years ago. Information services, especially companies with renewable revenues, look very promising. The software field has been our biggest single segment and will probably compose 20 to 25 percent of investments in our new fund. In the medical field, important areas are medical technology, device technology, and innovations that minimize a hospital stay or avoid surgery and therefore reduce the total cost. The toxic waste treatment field, biotechnology, and other service businesses are also promising.

The key to the venture capital business is finding the right investments. We decide which industries we want to invest in and organize our staff to focus on those industries, so that there are people within the firm who specialize in each industry. We invest in about 20 new companies every year. The process of generating opportunities and shrinking the leads down to 20 new investments is quite a job. Our staff must review thousands of companies to find 20 that meet our criteria. To begin with, we purchase about 5,000 Dun and Bradstreet company reports each year. When we find a prospect, we call the company for additional information. If they are worth visiting, a team is sent out to meet with the company. We visit about 2,000 different companies a year and find about 40 to 50 companies that are investment possibilities. Many of them are profitable; many do not need money. As a consequence, only about 20 investments result.

Our search effort is organized into teams. Each team works in a specific industry, spending 85 percent of its time in that industry. The goal is to find companies that have not been backed by venture capitalists before. One advantage of this approach is that we can often avoid the fairly competitive environment in the venture capital business, by finding companies where competition on price is not an issue. This strategy also gives us the opportunity to be a lead investor in each of these companies and to have more influence over their direction. We have achieved origination in about 66 percent of our investments; we find the other 33 percent through more traditional referral channels.

TABLE 5. Expected Loss Ratio

	Portfolio Mix	Number of Investments	Number of Failures
Start-Ups	25%	4	2
Development/ Revenue	25%	4	1
Profitable	50%	8	1
	100%	16	4 (25%)

Source: TA Associates

OUTLOOK FOR THE FUTURE

The future of the venture capital industry can best be examined by looking at the four key factors in the business: investment price, capital requirements, underlying growth, and exit prices.

The first is the investment price. Prices are fairly full today. The flow of new money into the venture industry is going to slow down in 1989. Although there is a huge amount of uninvested capital, I think we are moving into a better buying environment in 1989.

Second, the industry will be affected by the level of capital required by our portfolio companies. We have all become addicted to the amount of capital available in the venture business and, as a result, even successful companies tend to go through huge amounts of capital. Every time additional money is invested in a company, the original investment is diluted. If the flow of dollars into the venture industry declines, it will be necessary to slow down the burn rate over some of our companies to achieve greater returns. The venture culture has changed over the past 10 years from sweat equity where entrepreneurs would work in their garage and take a salary cut in exchange for equity, to entrepreneurs working in palatial buildings and taking handsome salaries as the venture capitalists continue to pump money in. Something will have to change in this equation if better rates of return are to be achieved.

The third factor, one that perhaps overwhelms all others, is the growth of the industries in which we are investing, and therefore, the growth of the individual companies. To a large extent, the success of the venture capital industry has been tied to the growth of the data processing industry. But the heyday is over in that industry: Over the next decade, the data processing industry will not grow as rapidly as it did from the late 1970s through the early 1980s. The growth for that industry is coming down and will stay down. To the extent that the venture capital industry is tied to the data processing industry, venture returns will be lower.

The final factor is the exit price. It is disturbing that private venture prices are increasing at a time (November 1988) when public prices have never been lower, and therefore, the discount for investing in private companies is really quite narrow. Hopefully, exit prices in the future will be more attractive than they have been the past few years.

CONCLUSION

Recently, the news about the venture industry has not been very positive. This is misleading. In 1983, there was nothing but good news about the venture business, but that news was based on investments made in the late 1970s; in fact, 1982-83 was the most difficult period to make new investments. The news today is based on the results of investments made in 1982 and 1983. It is not a reflection of what a venture capitalist can earn on investments made in 1988. When we know about the results of 1986, 1987, 1988, and 1989 (which will be available sometime in the early to mid-1990s), returns will be far better than the returns on investments made in the early 1980s.

Valuing Potential Investments—Part II

Franklin P. Johnson

The success of an investment program in venture capital partnerships depends on anticipating the performance of the venture partnership. This presentation addresses four issues that are useful in evaluating potential investments in venture firms: (1) performance measures; (2) the characteristics of a favorable partnership; (3) collateral benefits of investing in venture capital; and (4) how to choose a group in which to invest.

PERFORMANCE MEASURES

There are several ways to measure the performance of venture partnerships. Three of these ways are (1) portfolio performance, (2) partnership performance, and (3) return to the limited partners. The first alternative, portfolio performance, refers to the return on the money at risk, or the return on the series of individual investments. The second option, partnership performance, refers to how the whole partnership does, without regard to who invested the money in the partnership or who receives the return. Finally, the performance of the fund from the limited partners' perspective must also be considered, and in the end is the key measure.

To illustrate the difference between these three performance measures, I created a hypothetical portfolio, called Midas Partners, that is presumed to have started in 1978. The investments are categorized into six groups according to their returns: Category A, investments with investment multiples of 10 or more; Category B, multiples of 5 to 10; Category C, multiples of 3 to 5; Category D, multiples of 1.5 to 3; Category E, multiples of 0.5 to 1.5—the investments from which the money invested is returned, more or less; and Category F, multiples of less than 0.5—the complete losers. This portfolio is classified by the multiple return, not by the Internal Rate of Return (IRR), although IRR is shown for each investment, for the categories, and in total.

The first performance measure is the portfolio return. Table 1 shows a list of investments and their returns. The two investments in Category A had very high multiples—one was over 38 and the other was 10. Category B has four solid "workhorse" deals with investment multiples between 5 and 10. The primary performance of our hypothetical Midas fund occurred, as it often does, in categories A and B, with some contribution from investments in categories C and D. In combination, the deals in the first two categories produced slightly more than $80 million (total realization) from an investment of about $6 million. Investments in categories E and F were the losers. The IRR for the Midas portfolio is 42.5 percent.

The second performance measure is the partnership return. Table 2 shows the calculation of the partnership performance for Midas Partners. Performance at this level does not reflect the source of the capital or recipient of the distributions. In this example, the general partners put up 1 percent of the total capital and the limited partners put up 99 percent. In other partnerships, the general partners may provide 10 percent of the capital and the limited partners may put up 90 percent; the split is not important to the example. Table 2 shows the cash flow into and out of the fund. Cash flowed into the fund in three equal installments beginning in 1978, and the value, or cash, went out in six unequal payments beginning in 1983. The IRR on the partnership, before any carried interest but after the management fee, was 34 percent.

The third performance measure is the return to the limited partners. Table 3 shows the limited partners return factor, which is the decimal fraction of a limited partner's total investment returned by any deal or group of deals when distributed. The realization date is defined as the year in which the investment is available for distribution. FemtoTech, Inc.'s return of 1.83 indicates extraordinary performance; it means that the deal returned 1.83 times the limited partners' total investment. The rest of the investments returned considerably less. The sum of all the limited partner return factors is the amount received by the limited partners on their investments: In this case, the return is 5.23 times the money invested.

Table 3 also shows the timing of the money distributions by year. From 1983 to 1988, $77.6 million was returned to the limited partners on $14.8 million invested. The IRR is approximately 28 percent. A fund that had these returns, beginning

TABLE 1. Portfolio Performance: Midas Partners (Thousands of Dollars)

Company Name	Total Investment	First Investment Year	Last Investment Year	Realization Year	Total Realization	IRR	Investment Multiple
Category A (10 or more)							
FemtoTech, Inc.	$ 868	1978	1983	1985	$33,716	79.1%	38.8
HAL Computers	1,550	1978	1987	1988	15,500	49.7	10.0
Subtotal 2 companies	2,418				49,216	72.8	20.4
Category B (5.0 to 9.9)							
Peptide Labs, Inc.	688	1981	1985	1987	6,811	71.2	9.9
Unix Systems	772	1979	1981	1983	6,900	81.2	8.9
Sun Valley Semiconductor	1,389	1980	1982	1986	11,392	62.3	8.2
RSG Systems	945	1978	1983	1986	5,670	33.3	6.0
Subtotal 4 companies	3,794				30,773	54.8	8.1
Category C (3.0 to 4.9)							
Practical Software	566	1979	1983	1987	2,254	20.1	4.0
CryoConductance, Inc.	1,441	1980	1983	1985	5,244	37.5	3.6
Subtotal 2 companies	2,007				7,498	29.9	3.7
Category D (1.5 to 2.9)							
Motor Technology	681	1982	1983	1984	1,872	72.4	2.7
IPO Inc.	200	1979	1987	1987	526	27.4	2.6
Motion Visuals, Inc.	400	1978	1978	1984	930	15.3	2.3
Software, Inc.	1,072	1979	1979	1986	1,900	9.2	1.8
Subtotal 4 companies	2,353				5,228	18.2	2.2
Category E (0.5 to 1.4)							
Behavioral Systems	518	1978	1984	1986	690	4.2	1.3
Coffee Science	343	1979	1983	1984	200	-	0.6
Subtotal 2 companies	861				890	0.5	1.0
Category F (0.0 to 0.4)							
Descent Airlines, Inc.	1,064	1979	1980	1984	212	-	0.2
Combined Office Systems	563	1978	1979	1984	25	-	0.0
CAD Technology Ltd.	290	1980	1980	1983	0	-	0.0
Alpha Sciences	150	1978	1979	1980	0	-	0.0
Subtotal 4 companies	2,067				237	-	0.1
Total 18 companies	$13,500				$93,842	42.5%	7.0

Source: Asset Management Company

now, would be a strong performer, based on what we now believe about the business.

The three performance measures illustrated in Tables 1, 2, and 3 are different, which could mislead investors. I believe that the industry is moving toward the use of the return performance for limited partners as the primary determinant of performance; it is the one that means the most to investors.

Some firms try to predict how investments will do in the future, once the portfolio is nearly complete. We try to classify companies from A to F according to their expected performance. When the investments are first made, they are all As or Bs, naturally. As the real world sets in, however, the performance of some investments deteriorates. As new information becomes available, we revise our return forecasts and reclassify the companies. As long as the appropriate qualifications are communicated, a venture capital firm can properly give these estimates to its limited partners. These predictions are not perfect, however. For example, they do not address the problem of the J-curve or the quarterly evaluations. In fact, sometimes these estimates are only "guesstimates."

The most common current perspective on performance is obtained by using quarterly valuations. In our firm, quarterly valuations for private companies have four strictures on them: There must have been a new round of financing; they must involve a party, not in the original investor

TABLE 2. Performance Summary: Midas Partners (Thousands of Dollars)

Year	Cash In	Cash or Value Out
1978	$ 5,000	
1979	5,000	
1980		
1981	5,000	
1982		
1983		$ 6,900
1984		3,239
1985		38,960
1986		19,652
1987		9,591
1988		15,500
Total	$15,000	$93,842
Internal Rate of Return		34%

Source: Asset Management Company

group; the outside party must not have had a special deal—e.g., marketing rights—so that their investment is purely financial; and the company must have started operations. The last criterion adds additional reality to quarter-end valuation. There are times when companies in a hot field are bid up so fast that the valuations increase sharply before the companies can demonstrate the ability to ship, an event that may not occur in technology deals.

COLLATERAL BENEFITS

Although performance, if it can be measured, is helpful to investors in evaluating an investment, it is not the only determining factor. Some reasons for investing in venture capital are not directly related to the IRR or multiple returns. First, participation in venture capital provides additional knowledge. Venture capitalists must remain informed; they read many publications, attend many meetings, and cultivate informal contacts to learn more about emerging industries and companies. Investors will get high-quality research or collateral information from involvement in venture capital if they ask for the information or if the general partners have an organized way of presenting it to the limited partners.

Second, investors have the opportunity to build portfolios of growth stocks. Third, there are co-investment opportunities. Co-investment opportunities may be risky because few limited partners make thorough investigations separate from those of their general partners. Another consideration is that most venture capital firms do not like to treat one limited partner differently from another, and seldom promise co-investment rights. In negotiating a potential investment in a venture firm, some limited partners may separate themselves from the others by insisting on co-investment rights. This stricture might make it difficult for a partnership to promise these few limited partners co-investment rights. Co-investments do offer an opportunity to invest in later rounds of financing, but high prices are always a source of risk.

CHARACTERISTICS OF FAVORABLE PARTNERSHIPS

A good partnership relation is critical to the success of venture capital investments. There are several favorable characteristics of partnerships. As a matter of due diligence, all investors considering entering a partnership should make sure the general partners meet a set of criteria called the "Stanford Criteria" which were developed by the Stanford Investment Management Organization.

The first determination should be whether the partnership really acts like a partnership. Are decisions made to bring together the skills of all the partners or is it a series of individual entrepreneurs who make investment decisions and go through a pro forma approval at the partnership level?

Second, a potential investor must determine whether the partnership has the right amount of money for its strategy. A partnership that intends to do primarily start-ups and follow them through to conclusion must be small enough to make seed investments of between $100,000 and $1 million in a first round, and still have enough capital to follow through on later rounds. In this way, partnerships can support companies and attract other capital into them.

Third, a venture capital firm must have a strategy. Does it specialize in originating deals or getting involved in later stages? Does it specialize in certain business areas? Originating companies requires the ability to bring potential entrepreneurs, market ideas, and capital together. In addition, this type of venture capital firm must be sensitive to ideas and investment opportunities. Early-stage deals often result in the highest rates of return. Regardless of the stage, venture capital investments require substantial involvement with the companies that are potential investments.

The venture capital business is not really the investment business: rather, it is the business of building companies. The capital that partners

TABLE 3. Performance for Limited Partners: Midas Partners (Thousands of Dollars)

Company Name	1983	1984	1985	1986	1987	1988	Total	L. P. Return Factor
Category A (10 or more)								
FemtoTech, Inc.			$27,138				$27,138	1.83
HAL Computers						$12,694	12,694	0.85
Subtotal 2 companies			27,138			12,694	39,832	2.68
Category B (5.0 to 9.9)								
Peptide Labs, Inc.					$5,580		5,580	0.37
Unix Systems	$6,042						6,042	0.41
Sun Valley Semiconductor				$ 9,378			9,378	0.63
RSG Systems				4,716			4,716	0.32
Subtotal 4 companies	6,042			14,094	5,580		25,716	1.73
Category C (3.0 to 4.9)								
Practical Software					1,911		1,911	0.13
CryoConductance, Inc.			4,469				4,469	0.30
Subtotal 2 companies			4,469		1,911		6,380	0.43
Category D (1.5 to 2.9)								
Motor Technology		1,627					1,627	0.11
IPO, Inc.					459		459	0.03
Motion Visuals, Inc.		820					820	0.05
Software, Inc.				1,724			1,724	0.12
Subtotal 4 companies		2,447		1,724	459		4,630	0.31
Category E (0.5 to 1.4)								
Behavioral Systems				650			650	0.05
Coffee Science		198					198	0.01
Subtotal 2 companies		198		650			848	0.06
Category F (0.0 to 0.4)								
Descent Airlines, Inc.		210					210	0.02
Combined Office Systems		25					25	0.00
CAD Technology, Inc.							0	0.00
Alpha Sciences, Inc.							0	0.00
Subtotal 4 companies		235					235	0.02
Total 18 companies	$6,042	$2,880	$31,607	$16,468	$7,950	$12,694	$77,641	5.23
Limited Partner Return Factor (cumulative totals)	0.41	0.60	2.73	3.84	4.38	5.23		

Cash in = $14,850 ($4,950 on 1/78, $4,950 on 1/79, and $4,950 on 1/81)
Limited Partner IRR = 28%
L. P. Return Factor = Multiple of total limited partner investment returned.

Source: Asset Management Company

contribute to companies is an important element, but it is not the only element. Partners must also contribute a combination of work, energy, zeal, and enthusiasm to the companies. Those qualities are as important as the money.

The people involved in a venture capital operation are critical to successful partnerships. The partners' strengths should be emphasized and their role in the partnership should be clearly delineated. The number of partners and associates must be adequate to implement the strategy outlined by the general partners. Continuity of partners is also crucial to the success of the company; their experience is invaluable. Finally, there should be a plan for the development of new partners and associates, so that their talents are utilized and they are able to assume greater responsibilities and make significant contributions to the firm.

The final partnership characteristic that must be considered is whether the firm under consideration has a good relation with other venture firms. No fixed relation should exist with a series of firms that undertake co-investments, but it is important that contacts exist between the venture firm being considered and other firms in the field. Often, it is advantageous to have two or three firms in a deal to share the work and the risk. The venture is more likely to be successful because the partnership will have overcome the limits a single entity might have encountered.

There are exceptions to these characteristics, of course, depending on the situation. There are also some other considerations, primarily for partnerships involved in later stages of the venture development cycle. It is important that a balance exist between operating skills and venture capital or financial skills. Good management is important to a venture capital firm because it can make things happen in an investment. Conversely, experienced venture capital investors are important because they have a feel for the right prices, the correct structure, and the danger that may result from various terms and conditions written into a partnership agreement. A balance between management skills and venture capital skills is crucial.

MAKING THE DECISION

Once the characteristics of a partnership have been examined, the information collected must be analyzed to determine whether the potential partner will be able to carry out his or her mission. The risk is that the partnership will operate without a plausible scheme. An investor must be convinced that the firm has the elements necessary to make their strategy successful. If some of these criteria are missing, it is cause for concern.

Finally, it is vital that the venture capitalists themselves have a "joy of combat" that they can impart to their investments. Venture capital is not a detached, entirely rational business. Venture capitalists must believe in the companies they want to finance. Success often comes from determination, the desire to succeed, and the unwillingness to fail. If the enthusiasm and commitment are missing from a venture capital partnership, the risk becomes much greater. After making all of these rational analyses, intuition must guide the choice of a venture partnership: If it doesn't feel right, don't do it.

Question and Answer Session

QUESTION: Do you see any recovery in the initial public offering (IPO) market?

LANDRY: I am not terribly optimistic about the IPO market. There is a higher possibility of a recession in 1989. This would delay a recovery in the IPO market out to 1990. I am troubled by the record of growth in earnings of technology companies: they peaked in 1984, went into a real slump in late 1986, and now are coming out of that slump and perhaps have peaked again. The stocks peaked in 1983, anticipating that 1984 earnings peak, and then went down. They have not come up much. So, in terms of the earnings of these companies, there has been a complete cycle since l984, but we have not been paid, and that troubles me. We may have to wait another two years before these stocks improve if there is a recession in the technology sectors next year.

QUESTION: What are your views on strategic partnering as a strategy?

JOHNSON: Strategic partnering refers to the strategy of bringing in big companies to assist smaller companies. In some high-capital businesses like semiconductors and biotechnology, strategic partnering is an important element for a young company. It is helpful when capital requirements are substantial and when major international marketing is important to the success of the company.

QUESTION: It is generally believed that the big venture capital winners (25-fold or better) have occurred when market conditions were very receptive, especially for IPOs. Will similar gains be possible at the top of the next high-tech IPO cycle?

JOHNSON: It may be possible to find 25:1 winners, but most 100:1 winners are gone. The environment has changed. In the current market, there is plenty of money and a perception that it is imperative to start companies quickly and accelerate them into the marketplace. The public market conditions have a lot to do with determining the multiple, which itself is dependent on the ability to get going with a small amount of money.

LANDRY: I agree. In the current environment, investors cannot get into a deal at a low enough price; then because of the pressure to grow the companies fast, huge amounts of capital must be invested earlier in the cycles. Convex is a good example. It was a successful company, but it took huge amounts of capital. Investors put in money not only in the start-up round, but also in the second, third, and fourth rounds. In the end, they made three to four times on their money.

QUESTION: How do you decide when a venture does not warrant further investment?

LANDRY: If a company that is close to its plan comes back for more money, we will do some due-diligence to determine whether to give them more money, but we do not put it through the full screen. If, on the other hand, a company is behind plan and comes back for money, we put it through the same rigorous process as we would a new deal. If there is a problem, we turn the company over to someone in our office who closes it down.

JOHNSON: The routine delays are not really a problem; the surprises are what cause problems. Being behind plan is part of the process, but having no idea where you are is a problem.

QUESTION: Is there venture capital interest in new low-technology or no-technology areas?

JOHNSON: There may be. The critical question, however, is whether the company has a niche. Where there are fast-growing marketplaces that can be served by low or no technology, you have to determine whether there is anything unique about the company. In a high-tech area, the company may have an extraordinary group of technologists. In other areas, it may be extraordinary managers, well-proven people who can make a non-technology deal happen because they are terrific manufacturing people. There has to be some way to differentiate between companies, particularly if it is easy to start-up in that area. It is important to find the right market first; technology is really a secondary consideration, or at least only a co-consideration, to marketplace.

LANDRY: In my opinion, the best opportunities for growth are those created by technology—and they are also the ones that limit the competition for the longest period of time. That is not to say there are no opportunities in low-tech, but they tend to be scattered and miscellaneous.

QUESTION: Please outline the ownership percentages you normally attract in the earliest stages.

JOHNSON: For each company, we draw up a hypothetical financing plan that covers the life of the company, even if it is only a seed round. Typically, in a seed financing of $300,000 to $400,000, the reserve for future management and the entrepeneurs would often end up with over half the company. But that gets watered down pretty fast as the other rounds of financing come along. The goal is to provide enough incentive for everyone to stay excited about the deal.

LANDRY: As a general guideline, the rule is probably 50-50 on the initial capitalization. If an entrepreneur comes to us, it is going to be a 50-50 deal—maybe 40 to 50 percent for the entrepreneur and the other members of the management team. If we provide the original impetus, we may end up with more like 60 to 70 percent.

Does Venture Make Sense for the Institutional Investor? Part I

David F. Swensen[1]

Yale University has had an extraordinary experience with private equity investing. The private equity portfolio consists of commitments to both venture capital and leveraged buyout funds (LBOs). Since 1973 when the university made its first commitment to this area, the portfolio has earned 35 percent per year, compounded. The success stories of Yale and other early investors in venture capital and LBOs have attracted a flood of money to private equity transactions. In spite of this positive institutional experience, however, private equity investing is not necessarily appropriate for all institutional investors. In this presentation, I will examine the conceptual framework used at the university to evaluate these investments, the current market conditions in the venture capital industry, and some of the considerations involved in implementing a program of investing in private equities.

CONCEPTUAL FRAMEWORK

At Yale an enormous amount of time is spent working on asset allocation. In the book *Investment Markets*, Roger Ibbotson and Gary Brinson present the results of a study showing that over 90 percent of the variability in returns on institutional assets is determined by asset allocation; less than 10 percent is determined by security selection and market timing.[1] Unfortunately, asset allocation is more of an art than a science.

Yale's investment world is divided into five classes: domestic equity, domestic fixed-income, foreign equity, real estate, and private equity. The private equity portfolio consists of both leveraged buyouts and venture capital. These investment vehicles have been combined for two reasons. First, we must limit the number of asset classes. Second, the university believes that venture capital and leveraged buyouts share many characteristics. In particular, we select leveraged buyout funds that behave similarly to venture capital funds—groups with a strong value-added orientation that focus on enhancing the operations of the company rather than doing pure financial engineering.

The private equity asset class has three distinguishing characteristics: illiquidity, high expected risks and returns, and market imperfections.

Illiquidity. Private equity consists of extremely illiquid assets. Investments are generally made through the partnership format, which itself is very illiquid; partnership shares are difficult to sell at fair value. Furthermore, partnerships make investments in underlying assets that are illiquid. Because of this, it would be very difficult for a partnership to dispose of investments at anywhere close to fair value in a short time frame.

High Expected Risks and Returns. Private equity investments are characterized by high expected returns and high associated risks. The high return characteristic of private equity investing appeals to everyone—the flip side, of course, is that venture is an extremely risky asset. According to Roger Ibbotson, nominal returns in the venture industry were 30 percent per annum, and the standard deviation on those returns was 86 percent per annum over the period 1959-85. Another data source shows that inflation-adjusted returns in the private equity area over the period 1946-87 were around 23 percent, with a standard deviation of 56 percent. In statistical terms, that means that there is an approximately two-thirds probability that the returns will range between minus 33 percent and plus 79 percent in a given year—an extraordinary dispersion.

The historical risk-return trade-off for Yale's different asset classes is shown in Figure 1. Venture capital is much riskier and has much higher inflation-adjusted expected returns than marketable securities and real estate, which comprise the university's other investment vehicles. Figure 2 shows two Markowitz mean-variance efficient frontiers, one with venture and one without. The points along the frontier represent the most efficient combinations of assets.

---

[1]With research assistance from Tim Sullivan.

[2]Ibbotson, Roger G. and Gary P. Brinson, *Investment Markets*, New York, NY: McGraw Hill, 1987.

FIGURE 1. Asset Classes Risk and Return Characteristics

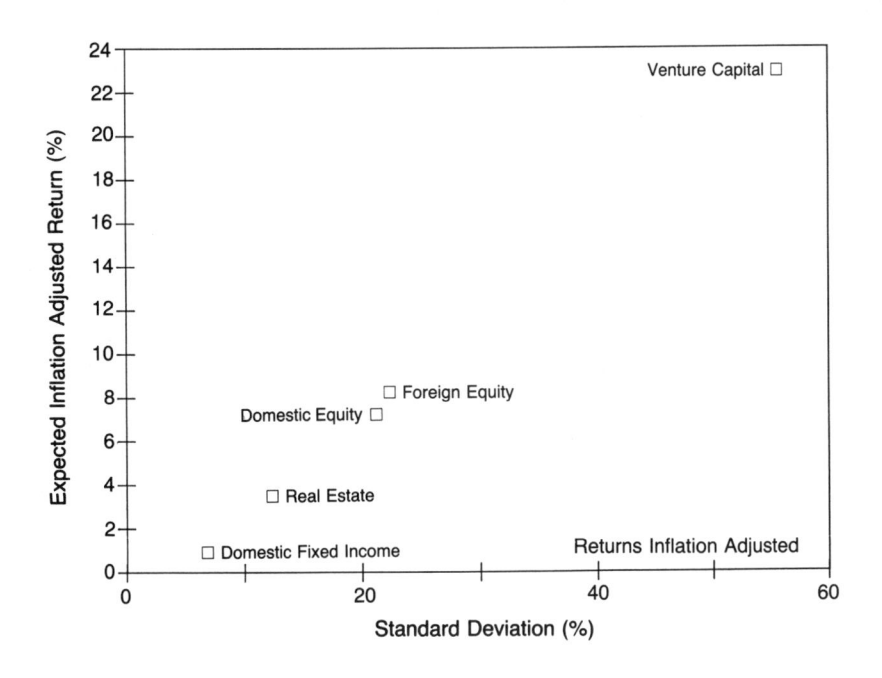

Source: Yale Investments Office Estimates

FIGURE 2. Efficient Frontiers With and Without Venture Capital

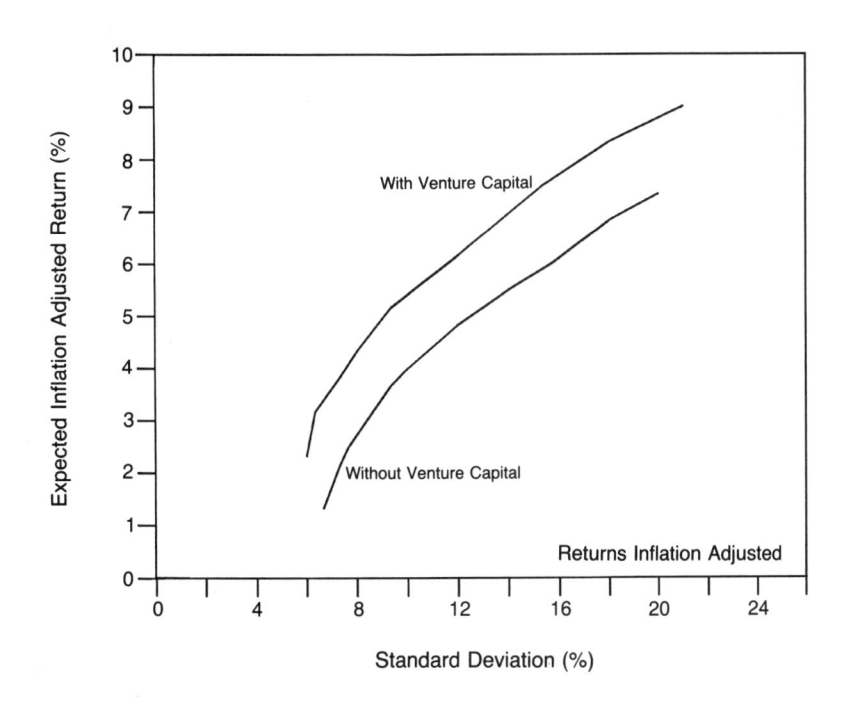

Source: Yale Investments Office Estimates

In this context, efficiency means that a portfolio provides the maximum return for a given level of risk or the minimum risk for a given level of return. The lower frontier consists of the basic set of portfolio assets: domestic equity, domestic fixed-income, foreign equity, and real estate. In the second frontier, the model allows the possibility of a 10 percent allocation to venture. The addition of venture to the basic portfolio results in an extraordinary change in the opportunity set. At any given level of risk, expected returns increase by more than one full percentage point simply by allowing the portfolio to include allocation to private equities.

The statistical diversification found in the Markowitz mean-variance analysis should not be overemphasized. Quantitative aspects of private equity must be combined with qualitative consideration of the investments. Private equity acts much like public market equity securities. In terms of a continuum, large-capitalization stocks could be placed on the left, small-capitalization stocks somewhere in the middle, and private equity on the far right. Over long holding periods, we determined that these equity classes had the following characteristics: Large-capitalization stocks had real returns of 8 percent, small-capitalization stocks had real returns of 12 percent, and private equity had real returns in the neighborhood of 20 percent. Standard deviations increased comparably: large-capitalization stocks around 21 percent, small-capitalization stocks around 32 percent, and private equity about 50 percent. The correlations were interesting as well. Moving from the large-capitalization stocks to private equity, there is increasingly less correlation with other assets, implying increasing statistical diversification.

Those statistical relations are instructive, but they do not explain what is really going on in private equity investing. One can expect more risk—but not substantial diversification—relative to other equity holdings in a portfolio. The basic factors that influence publicly traded equity securities also influence investments in the private equity market. One may argue that, in the early stages, successful venture capital investments create value that is independent of what is going on in the public markets. Ultimately, however, values in the venture capital market are dependent on valuations in the exit markets; because of this, one cannot expect private equity to diversify risk vis-a-vis publicly traded equity securities.

Market Imperfections. The private equity market is characterized by market imperfection. In a relatively efficient market, like the U.S. stock market, a passive approach to making investment decisions may be sensible. Over time, the best active managers in the domestic equity markets are only able to exceed market benchmark returns by two or three percentage points. It is most likely, in the zero-sum game of the domestic equity markets, that because trades incur transaction costs and create market impact, performance will fail to match market indexes. The absolute converse is true in an inefficient market. A passive approach which involves making allocations to a broad range of market participants is a recipe for disaster. In inefficient markets, it is very important to take an active approach, and to select the best investment opportunities.

When evaluating the appropriateness of private equity for a particular institutional portfolio, the asset class should be considered in conjunction with the overall assets and liabilities of the institution. For the private equity class to be attractive, the institution must have an extremely long time horizon and high return requirements. The long-term time horizon is necessary because investments are illiquid, making disposition prior to maturity difficult. It is also important to be able to look through cycles in the private equity market. If commitments are made for a relatively short period of time, they may be focused in a period of bad vintages and not continue into years in which the returns are superior. The long-term horizon is necessary to capture both the peaks and the unfortunate valleys in investment experience.

CURRENT MARKET CONDITIONS

In the recent past, there have been more dollars committed to the venture market, more partnerships created, and larger funds formed. (See Figures 3, 4, and 5.) The intuitive, and probably correct, conclusion is that these three trends have caused a lowering of returns in the venture industry. I predict that we will see even more dollars committed to the venture industry, even more partnerships created, and even lower returns in the future.

The primary sources of institutional dollars include public and private pensions, direct corporate investment, insurance companies, endowments, and foundations. According to a recent issue of *Pensions and Investment Age*,[3] the top 1,000 pension plans have approximately $1.3 trillion in assets; 1 percent of

---

[3]*Pensions and Investment Age,* January 23, 1989

FIGURE 3. Venture Capital Funds Average Size

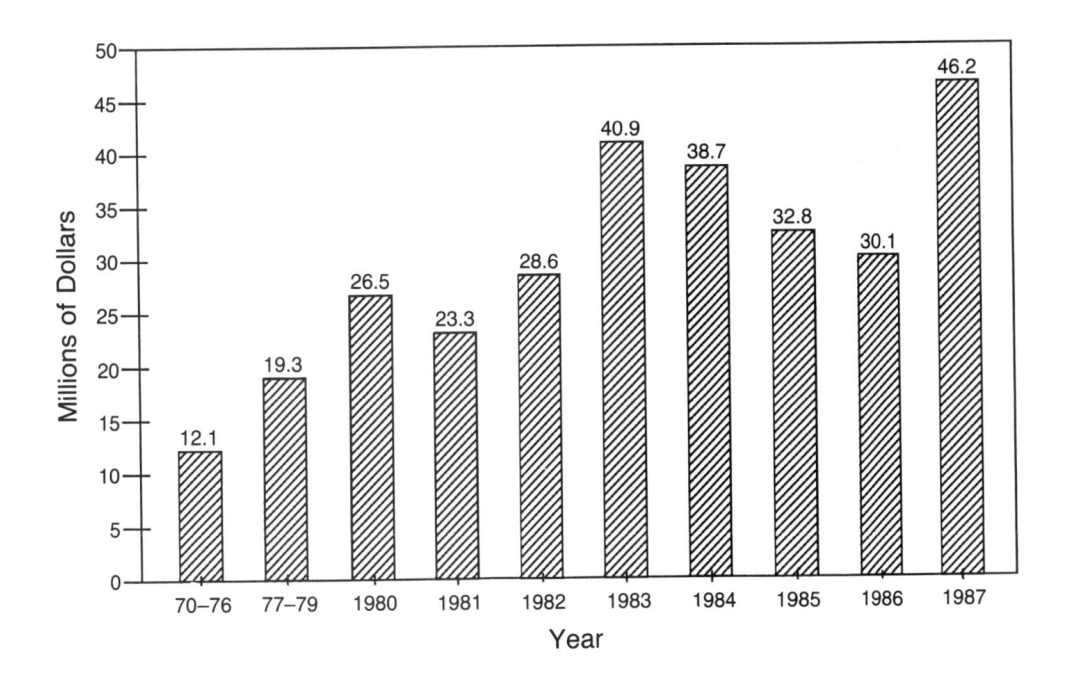

Year	Millions of Dollars
70–76	12.1
77–79	19.3
1980	26.5
1981	23.3
1982	28.6
1983	40.9
1984	38.7
1985	32.8
1986	30.1
1987	46.2

Source: Venture Economics

these pension assets amounts to $13 billion. Clearly, 1 percent is not a meaningful allocation for the pension community, but the potential investment is absolutely staggering to the venture community. In competitive markets, pecuniary externalities are not a significant factor; the actions of any economic participant cannot affect price or supply or demand. But in an extremely illiquid market, like the venture market, the external pecuniary factors can be enormous. A dramatic increase in institutional funds available to venture capitalists will inevitably reduce returns. Such a reduction may ultimately discourage entrepreneurship in the venture community. In the markets for publicly traded securities, if there were a huge inflow of funds, there would be a relatively quick adjustment process. In the venture market, a huge inflow of funds would result in a long, painful adjustment process.

PRACTICAL IMPLEMENTATION

There are several ways to implement a program of venture investments. You could make direct company investments, direct investments in venture partnerships, or a combination of the two. Instead of making direct decisions, you could hire someone to assemble your portfolio. In any case, in structuring venture investments, you must consider several diversifying characteristics: time of partnership formation—a very important type of diversification; stage of investment; partnership characteristics; and geographic specialization—an overrated type of diversification.

Several issues must be addressed in creating a venture investment program. First, you must be extremely selective in funding partnerships. It is exciting to put together a new investment program, but the initial enthusiasm may cause some people to put the money to work too quickly. I recently heard of a fund that made commitments to 40 groups in an 18-month period. It is difficult to imagine that there were 40 groups worthy of funding in the past 18 months. Investors must be selective.

Second, there is a limited universe of venture capital funds. Many top funds have never accepted institutional money, others are closed to new participants, and many of those accepting new partners take limited amounts of money. A new entrant into venture investing may well be selecting from a universe of funds that excludes the most experienced, most successful venture capitalists.

Finally, many new entrants into venture investing

FIGURE 4. Venture Capital Returns by Fund Vintage Through 12/31/87

Year	Annualized Return (%)
70–76	20.8
77–79	31.6
1980	20.6
1981	9.3
1982	0.0
1983	7.4
1984	1.7
1985	5.0
1986	1.9

Source: Venture Economics

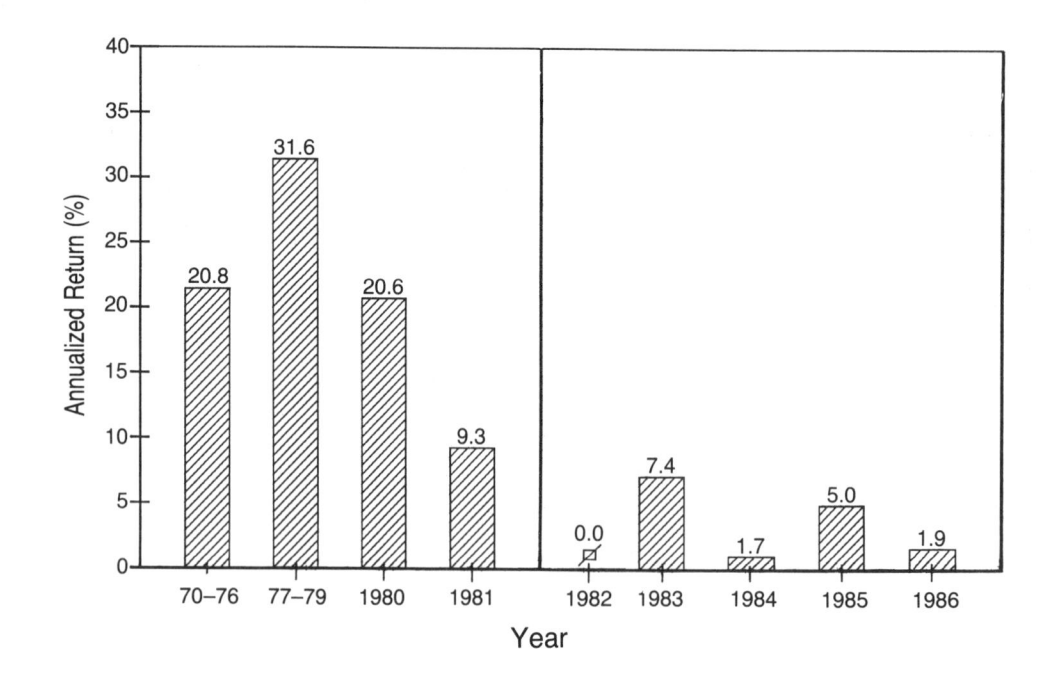

FIGURE 5. Capital Commitments to Independent Venture Capital Firms

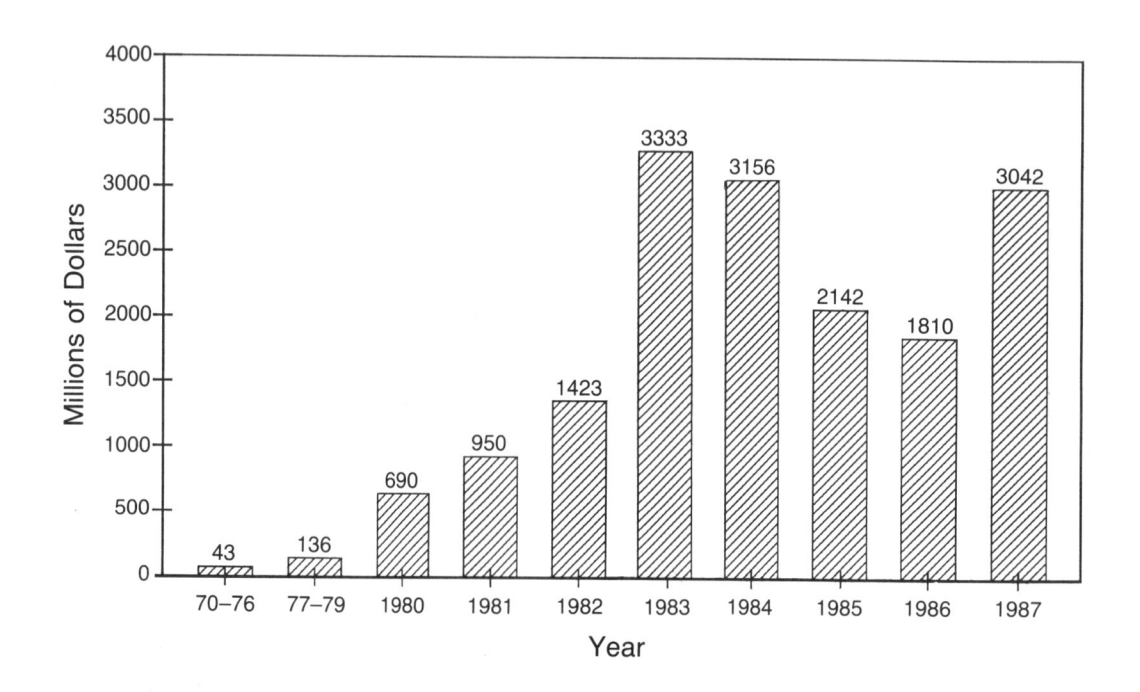

Year	Millions of Dollars
70–76	43
77–79	136
1980	690
1981	950
1982	1423
1983	3333
1984	3156
1985	2142
1986	1810
1987	3042

Source: Venture Economics

lack a long-term commitment. In recent years, a number of portfolios were created by institutions that wanted to invest in the venture industry, and then, for whatever reason, lost interest just as they were becoming familiar with the market, and several months later were out in the market trying to sell their limited partnership interests to other investors. This is a serious problem because investments focused in relatively short periods are not diversified across the venture cycle. It is possible to hit the cycles right, but it is far more likely that you will invest at the top (attracted by recent high returns) and then turn around and sell at the bottom (discouraged by recent low returns).

CONCLUSION

Returning to the basic question of whether venture capital makes sense for institutional investors, the answer is a qualified yes. I would caution investors to consider the program in the context of their assets and liabilities, and not be seduced by historical performance statistics. Institutions should consider a venture program only if they are comfortable expecting much lower returns from the venture capital community in the future. The institutions involved should recognize the pitfalls in venture investing, especially some of the externalities that they may be responsible for creating.

Does Venture Make Sense for the Institutional Investor? Part II

Greta E. Marshall, CFA

I am going to discuss the institutional perception of the characteristics of venture capital and how that fits in with the investment objectives of institutional investors; comment on the institutionalization of the venture capital market, with emphasis on the role that the public funds appear to be playing; and comment on whether venture capital makes sense for the institutional investor. Before discussing these issues, I would like to review the evolution of the venture capital market.

THE EVOLUTION OF THE VENTURE CAPITAL MARKET

I divide the venture capital market into two periods: Before Institutions and After Institutions. The breakpoint is about 1970.

Before the 1970s, the venture capital market was mostly left to wealthy individuals, for certain very good reasons. First, venture capital was in some ways a tax shelter, which was not typically attractive to the tax-exempt institutional market. Second, venture capital was considered a high-risk investment—often attracting individuals who had already made a fortune in high-risk endeavors. Third, there was less of an agency effect—the fact that pension fund investors manage other people's money—in the industry than there is today. Most of the monies were invested directly by the wealthy individuals, or at least by their agents. These individuals were more closely involved in the whole process than, say, pension funds are today as agents for an amorphous mass of pensioneers.

There are several characteristics of venture capital that attracted institutions to the area before institutionalization. First, venture capital is a long-term investment. It is also a high-return, albeit a high-risk, investment, but that is not, in my opinion, a hurdle for the typical private pension plan. Venture capital is also a management- and analysis-intensive investment which requires a high level of analytical expertise. Because most pension funds did not have that expertise in-house, they had to hire outside people, in one form or another, to make venture capital investments. Nevertheless, it was worth the effort for some institutions because there were inefficiencies in the market that could be turned into attractive returns.

The characteristics of venture capital investments are consistent with the investment objectives of many institutions. The investment objectives of most institutions, particularly pension funds, should be very long-term; the average life of the liabilities of a typical pension plan is 20 to 25 years. Furthermore, high levels of volatility should not be a drawback to pension plans. Because pension funds have no immediate need for liquidity on a short-term basis, long-term volatility should simply represent attractive buying opportunities for those funds.

There are several tax-related issues surrounding venture capital investments. First, wealthy individuals found investments in venture capital attractive because of the tax write-offs. (Investors are able to write off the companies that fail.) Some of those write-offs were very attractive to individuals who could use them as tax shelters. Much of this tax-related attraction has changed with the revision of the U.S. tax code.

Another effect lies in the fact that venture capital investments are appraised assets. In general, the pricing of appraisal portfolios is not as volatile as the pricing of market-priced portfolios. Given the new regulations on pricing pension portfolios and reporting those liabilities on balance sheets, appraisal assets such as real estate and venture capital will be much more attractive to pension funds in the future.

The fee structure in venture capital partnerships is not going to be acceptable to institutions. When venture capital funds were much smaller, the 20 percent carried interest paid to the general partners was a substantial but not outrageous amount of money. But it is very difficult to see how a 20 percent carried interest paid to general partners makes any sense at all in a $1 billion fund or even in a $500-million fund. If the venture capital funds want to attract institutional business—and there is some evidence that they do—investors will require a fee structure that is fair and reasonable.

THE INSTITUTIONALIZATION OF VENTURE CAPITAL

The industry has changed since institutions became interested in the venture capital market. There have been some unattractive consequences as a result of institutionalization. The first problem is that institutions are typically quite large. In general, they have much greater resources than any of the wealthy individuals who might be investing independently around the country. The size of institutions affects their decisions to invest in venture capital.

It is difficult to see how investments can be rationally made when one fund dominates an investment medium. For example, the California Public Employees' Retirement Fund (CALPERS)—which is now roughly a $50-billion fund—has some serious issues to consider before committing money to venture capital. When I was at CALPERS, I recommended that venture capital ought to be 5 percent of the fund. Five percent of $50 billion is $2.5 billion—probably more than is committed to the venture capital business in any one year if the leveraged buyout funds are eliminated. It is more than all of the money invested in the venture business in 1985. It is also a very large portion—approximately 10 percent—of the total amount of money committed to the venture capital industry.

CALPERS chose not to invest in venture capital. The advisory board thought that venture capital was a wonderful idea for pension funds, but they did not think that investing in venture capital was valuable for a fund as large as CALPERS, for two reasons. First, they thought that an investment under 5 percent was inappropriate because investments of less than 5 percent do not get enough attention and, in the long term, do not have a major impact on return. Second, a 5 percent investment on behalf of the California funds was clearly too large a commitment for one fund to make to what they perceived to be a very small industry.

Another problem with the institutionalization of venture capital is the combination of funds with different characteristics. In particular, the leveraged buyout (LBO) funds should not be categorized as venture capital. One reason that venture capital is so attractive for pension funds is that their liabilities rise and fall with the long-term growth of the economy, and I think that the long-term growth of the economy is best served by equity investments in emerging new companies, not leveraged buyouts of established firms.

There are other investments that are misclassified as venture capital. The venture capital industry has expanded from its original high-tech orientation into other fields, for example retail funds. It is much harder to defend a pension investment in a chocolate chip cookie company, for example, or in a teeny-bopper dress retailer than in the high-tech industry. The institutional movement into venture capital has been accompanied by considerable confusion about what venture capital really is and the purpose of venture capital in the development of new ventures. In my opinion, these changes have hurt the industry.

The third effect relating to the institutionalization of venture capital is the agency effect. The agency effect refers to the types of decisions that pension fund managers make because they are not investing their own money when they invest in venture capital pools—or, in fact, in any investment; they are investing other people's money. The agency relation affects the types of investments that pension fund managers choose. These managers have almost no motivation or incentive to take risk, particularly managers of the public funds. Most public fund employees are civil servants or, increasingly, contract employees who do not receive any incentive compensation. These people will not benefit in any meaningful way from an investment whose returns are exceptionally good. On the other hand, if the returns are very bad, they will end up in front of the legislature in public hearings. Thus, the agency effect will have an impact on the type of venture capital funds selected by institutional investors and, consequently, on the returns earned on those funds.

There is one other aspect of venture capital investing in the public sector that I find particularly distasteful: economic targeting. Most public funds are required to invest a portion—frequently a substantial portion of the venture capital allocation—within their own states. This is one way that states are trying to reach the large pools of pension money and use that money to build the economy of their own state. I think it is a mistake to force money into a specific region. In fact, it has been shown that the general purpose funds which were opportunistic and invested throughout the country have generally outperformed other funds. Restricting the investments of the public funds to in-state funds is very damaging, both from the point of view of the long-term economic consequences to the country and from the perspective of a rational and realistic venture capital industry.

CONCLUSION

I think venture capital makes sense for institutional investors, but I think institutional investors may not make sense for venture capital. It is very important that those of us who are involved in the industry, on both sides, try to minimize the damages that will be caused by institutionalization. These problems will arise from pressure to target economic areas, the agency effect, the conservatism that will subtly influence investments, and the complications arising from the size of many of these pension funds. The irony of the size problem is that there is too much money, not too little.

There are many investment opportunities begging for investment capital, and they present an opportunity to improve the U.S. economic position in the world. The problem is that as the funds grow larger, there will be a tendency to concentrate in fewer companies. Venture capitalists will have the same problem that portfolio managers have in managing large equity portfolios (portfolio managers have to concentrate more money in fewer stocks, because one person can only follow a limited number of stocks). There are also consequences of giving too much money to too few good opportunities. Too much money is the worst problem that venture capitalists can have, because too much money undermines their incentive to find less costly and more efficient methods. The end result of too much money, too early, is a failed venture.

Question and Answer Session

QUESTION: How should an institution go about investing in venture capital? Should it consider a fund of funds, direct investment, or the partnership route?

MARSHALL: The answer depends on the institution's expertise in the venture capital industry, the desired level of involvement, and the amount of time it wants to devote to venture capital. If the institution has no expertise and does not want to spend any time, the only option is to hire someone who produces a fund of funds. At the other end of the spectrum, if the institution has the expertise and is willing to commit the resources to venture investments, it may make direct investments. My philosophy is a little different than most of the speakers in these proceedings: I recommended that CALPERS buy every reasonable partnership that came along, plus some directs, and some fund of funds. I recommended the indexed approach because it is not clear to me that we are better at picking venture capital managers or partnerships than plan sponsors are at picking investment managers. Nor is it clear to me that we, as plan sponsors, are any better at timing our entrance into the venture capital market than we are at timing our entrance and exit from the traditional stock and bond markets.

SWENSEN: If I were starting from scratch, I would work with a fund of funds. After the portfolio had been created, I might make partnership investments directly. The initial contact with a fund manager would allow me to learn a lot about the industry and piggyback on some of the manager's expertise. It is almost impossible for an institutional investor to make direct company investments. The main problem is that we do not compensate our people at anywhere near the levels that the venture capital community does. If we get people who are good at making direct investments, we run the risk of losing them to a firm that pays more money, leaving us with companies that we cannot follow in our portfolio. So I would avoid that route entirely.

QUESTION: Please describe the criteria that you use to decide which partnerships you will invest in and how you manage those investments over time.

SWENSEN: The most important criterion is the quality of the people involved in the venture partnership. That is a very difficult thing to assess. Among other things, we look for people who have had reasonable success working together as a partnership. Once a relation is established, we try to keep informed on what the partnerships are doing. We attend annual meetings and we meet our venture capitalists once a year at their offices. I would like to stress how important it is to create a long-term relation with your partners. We prefer partnerships that make us feel that we are full partners with the venture capitalists, not limited partners. In return, we tend to fund our venture capital firms for long periods of time.

QUESTION: What type of guidelines do you use in establishing venture capital partnerships?

MARSHALL: I think the most important covenants are the ones that minimize the conflict of interest. Personally, I do not like investment management fees that go directly to the partners; the fees should come through the venture capital partnership, so that partners concentrate on finding the best investments for the fund rather than on their private fee income. The venture capitalists should not get paid unless the limited partners get paid a reasonable rate of return—in excess of what they could have gotten in the public markets.

SWENSEN: For our private equity investing, we feel strongly that the interests of the general partners should coincide with those of the limited partners. If interests do not coincide, we move on to the next opportunity; we do not try to solve it by structuring the documents differently.

QUESTION: If returns are higher and competition is less intense in smaller venture capital funds—e.g., funds in the $20 to $30 million range—shouldn't institutional investors invest in smaller funds?

MARSHALL: I think that returns form a continuous spectrum similar to the equity returns across stocks with different capitalizations (e.g., large-capitalization versus small-capitalization companies). When the venture capital industry gets the quality of performance data that is currently available for the publicly traded markets, I think one will find that the smaller funds, comprising mostly the smaller, early-stage investments, will have the highest returns. The real difficulty is in being able to find those funds. For that reason, I advocate an indexed approach. I do not advocate buying every fund that comes along, only those that have an acceptable philosophy, qualified people, and a reasonable process for making investments. In addition, the funds must charge reasonable fees, and share returns on an equitable basis. Because pension funds have a longer time horizon than other investors, they can afford to disperse their funds over these very small partnerships and take a much longer time horizon. It is very difficult for large public funds to invest in the smaller funds.

SWENSEN: My principal concern about small funds is the relation between the limited partners and the general partners. It is not good for either the general partner or the limited partner to have one particular source of funds dominate the fund. We commit at least $5 to $10 million to each of our venture funds; that is too large a piece of many of the smaller funds.

MARSHALL: I believe in using a very disciplined quantitative or mechanical approach to selecting stocks. In our small-capitalization equity portfolios—both at CALPERS and Deere—we held upwards of 500 different companies. The same thing can be done in the venture capital area. It is not possible to develop long-term relations with the general partners using this approach, but I do not put as high a value on developing relations as Mr. Swensen does.

QUESTION: Please comment on the fee structures for partnerships and fund-of-funds managers.

MARSHALL: I have the same problem with fees in this area that I have almost everywhere. The fee structures that we are dealing with—and that the venture capitalists would like to tell you are "standard" for the industry—were developed during a period when funds were much smaller, and the majority of investors were individuals. This structure is not appropriate for institutional investors. The institutional investor, acting on behalf of his or her beneficiaries, has an absolute obligation to negotiate reasonable fees. I do not consider the fees reasonable in the venture capital area—that is, the 1 or 2 percent asset management fee and the 20 percent carry. The fees in the LBO area are even worse. Fees should only cover reasonable expenses and the carried interest should be the vehicle for rewarding the general partners.

SWENSEN: I agree that there are a lot more problems in the LBO fee structures than there are in the venture structures. The system generally has worked quite well. In venture partnerships, the interests of the general partners usually coincide with those of the limited partners, and that is certainly not true in many of the LBO partnerships.

Terms for Investing—Part I

Richard J. Testa

There are numerous terms that are of interest to people investing in the venture capital industry. In this presentation, I will discuss the terms that have a direct impact on investment results. Exhibit 1 depicts key provisions and related issues in a hypothetical venture capital limited partnership.

HISTORY OF TERMS

The terms of investing in venture capital have evolved over time. Before 1946, individuals and families dominated the venture capital markets. Each deal was done on its own merit. The investor acquired the securities for his or her own account, so the source of capital was both the record and beneficial holder. There was no intermediation; there was no need for distributions. Returns could be calculated at the time a company became public.

The industry begin to change radically in 1946. The dominant investment vehicle became the professionally managed corporate entity. Generally, it was a nondiversified, closed-end investment company that sold either on an exchange or in the over-the-counter market, invariably at a discount to net asset value. The corporation had an indefinite life, and the managers had no obligation to distribute returns. The corporate format did not work well with institutional investors, however. American Research is a good example of a fund from that period. In 1972, American Research—a highly successful vehicle—was forced out of existence because the corporate format did not allow, at least on a tax-efficient basis, distributions, realization, and returns.

Beginning in the early 1960s, the format changed from corporate entities to partnerships. The 10-year life partnership is an extraordinarily efficient business and tax vehicle. It lends itself very well to tax-wise distributions in kind and in cash. The 10-year or occasionally shorter life forces the manager to show results, at the risk of not being funded for future partnerships.

During the 1978-82 period, a plethora of new groups came into the industry, generally showing promise, but not necessarily results. Typically, a 1978 venture partnership was capitalized at a $10 to $20 million level and had two or three partners. Everyone demanded the going terms: a 2.5 percent management fee and a 20 percent carried interest. There were some examples of pressure for reductions in the 2.5 percent fee, but they were very modest. There were also examples of a carried interest greater than 20 percent, but again, these situations were not typical.

CURRENT TERMS

In 1988, 10 years later, those terms are still the norm, but many of them are being challenged. The most hotly contested issues are the 2.5 percent management fee and 80-20 carried interest fees. There is an occasional assault on the amount of the management fee, but the challenge is subtle. People do not argue with 2.5 percent when the fund is only $20 million. But when the fund is a megafund, with $200 to $600 million under management and some of the earlier partnerships in a near to final liquidation mode, it might be appropriate to question whether 2.5 percent of committed capital on a later fund is appropriate.

There is also pressure on the carried interest terms. Ten years ago, it was very common to compute the carried interest on all income, including income from short-term money market investments. With the advent of double-digit inflation and short-term money market account returns approaching 20 percent, some people began to question whether the operating venture capitalist was entitled to a 20 percent carry on the 15 percent earned on a money market account. These objections led to discussions of alternative terms, including allocation solely to the limited partners of short-term money market gross, short-term money market net, or no specific differentiation. There was also the development of a gradual take-down by the venture capital partnership. To improve the rates of return as shown by the venture capital partnership, the capital was taken down on an "as needed" basis. That is, for example, a blended rate between 5 percent money market and 30 percent on venture investment was not used.

Establishing the amount of the fee or the carried

interest split is only the beginning of the analysis. One must also decide when to allocate the 20 percent to the general partner. Is it from day one? Is it from the date of the first return of capital? Or from the date that there was a return of capital plus some imputed rate of return? Allocation is one part of the analysis; distribution is much more important. Distribution is related to what has been called a make-up provision, or restoration provision, or return of deficit capital accounts—it all means the same thing. From the partnership's first day to its last, there should be exactly a 20 percent allocation of profits and a 20 percent distribution to the fund's general partners. It is possible to have under- or overdistributions. In October 1987, some funds that made early distributions to general partners before October 17, but had not yet returned original contributed capital to limited partners, found themselves in a position of overdistribution. In these cases, the funds had to use the restoration deficit provision to rectify the situation. Five to eight years ago, this was not a factor; today, this term is mandatory.

With the structural change that has occurred in the funding process, more attention is being paid to those terms where problems may develop or where an enhancement of returns can be made. When returns are 25 percent or more, it is very easy to be cavalier about the extra 0.5 percent of return—it is irrelevant. Because returns from the venture industry are going down, it is important to look at ways to enhance the returns without damaging the industry or the general partners.

Ten years ago, a typical venture firm was set up as a single limited partnership with two or three individual general partners, and no other provisions. Today, it is more common to use the two-tier partnership. The main partnership is the investing fund; the general partner is structured as another limited partnership. The individual general partners are one step removed from the fund partnership. This structure has many operational advantages. Over the past few years, however, it has caused problems because some people have not paid enough attention to the agreement between the general partnership and the limited partnership. This is where the major issues are found: vesting, control of operations, admission of new partners, dissolution of the firm, and removal of partners. In the close-knit industry of 10 to 15 years ago, the notion of a fight among general partners was heresy. Today, issues like continuity and perpetuity must be addressed. They should be addressed by the general partners themselves, and on a periodic basis by the limited partners. Many issues are not apparent in the straightforward reading of the fund limited partnership agreement, and indeed, 10 years ago were not addressed there either. In today's environment, these issues must be addressed. For example, failure to address the issue of retirement is an opportunity for mischief because many well-established firms go into second or third generation of general partners. Before making an investment, it is important to look at the people, and then the terms embedded in the partnership agreements.

EXHIBIT 1. Summary of Venture Capital Terms: Ad-Venture Capital Fund, L.P.

	Provision	Summary	Issues
1.	Entity	Ad-Venture Capital Fund, L.P. (the "Fund").	—
2.	Purpose	To produce superior long-term returns by investing in emerging growth companies.	This general statement of purpose leaves open the issue of whether there will be any restrictions on the Fund's investment activities. Certain investors will seek to impose bans or limits (e.g., no more than 10 percent of capital) with respect to activities such as investments in leveraged buyouts or public companies. Investors may also seek to prohibit the Fund from investing in other investment vehicles, on the theory that the investors could make such investments directly without compensating the General Partner. The Fund will resist these restrictions because they limit flexibility and can be difficult to structure.
3.	General Partner	Ad-Venture Capital Partners, L.P. (the "General Partner"). The general partners of the General Partner are John Doe, Richard Roe, and Harry Hoe (the "Individual General Partners").	The Fund's conventional, two-partnership format raises the following issues: (a) *Access*. Will investors in the Fund have access to the General Partner's partnership agreement? Such access would permit a review of many important issues, such as vesting of the Individual General Partners' interests, admission of new Individual General Partners, removal of existing Individual General Partners, and restrictions on activities of Individual General Partners (such as a requirement that the Individual General Partners devote substantially all of their business time to the affairs of the Fund or a prohibition on certain transactions between the Individual General Partners and the Fund). (b) *Participation*. Are any persons other than the Individual General Partners participating in the General Partner? "Angels" or "sponsors" who have agreed to provide financial or other up-front assistance frequently become partners in the General Partner and thereby participate in the "carried interest." This sharing may be perceived as diluting the effectiveness of the carry as an incentive for the Individual General Partners.
4.	Limited Partnership Interests	$100 million to be offered, with a minimum of $5 million for each investor. The General Partner reserves the right to increase the offering to $125 million.	The amount of the Fund's capital can become an issue if the investors question the ability of the Individual General Partners to put the money to work effectively. Investors will generally prefer lower rather than higher required minimum capital contributions. In some cases, however, high minimums can signal that a Fund is a "hot" deal.
5.	General Partner's Contribution	The General Partner will make a contribution equal to 1 percent of the Fund's total capital.	Although a 1 percent contribution has been the industry standard, issues increasingly arise in two areas: (a) *Amount*. Particularly with respect to larger funds ($50 million and up), the Individual General Partners may seek to make less than a 1 percent contribution. (b) *Type of Contribution*. The Individual General Partners may seek to make some of their contributions in the form of promissory notes to the Fund; investors will

Provision	Summary	Issues
		usually prefer cash. New tax rules in this area are imminent.
6. Minimum for Closing	Commitments for $50 million in Limited Partnership interests must be received prior to an initial closing.	Amount of capital required for an initial closing may become an issue if investors become concerned about investing in a Fund that is too small to support an active venture program. Constraints on subsequent closings often become a topic for negotiation. Investors prefer to limit subsequent closing to a fixed period (e.g., 60 to 180 days) after initial closing. Investors in initial closing will insist that organizational expenses and service fees for first year be allocated pro rata to capital, regardless of time when investor comes on board.
7. Payment of Subscriptions	One-third at closing with no further calls during first year. Maximum of additional one-third callable during second year. Balance payable when called thereafter within period ending four years from closing.	Biggest issue with respect to timing of capital calls is tension between desires for flexibility and a fixed schedule. The General Partner generally prefers flexible approach, which (i) assures funds will be available as needed and (ii) enhances the Fund's R.O.I. to investors. Some investors will insist that the General Partner's flexibility be limited by staged drawdowns, which cannot be accelerated but may be deferred. Some investors prefer a fixed schedule of drawdowns, which enables them to predict cash management requirements with greater certainty. The current trend is toward more flexibility.
8. Term	Ten years.	The General Partner prefers a longer term; investors frequently want to limit to 10 years or less. Compromise often sets an initial term but permits extensions; latter often require either (i) approval or non-disapproval by investors or (ii) satisfaction of certain conditions (e.g., at least 30 percent of Fund's assets in non-marketable securities; extension permitted for wind-up).
9. Allocation of Profit and Loss	80 percent to all Partners on the basis of capital contributions and 20 percent to the General Partner.	Although 80/20 has become industry "standard," many variations are possible: (a) 80/20 allocation of *all* items of income, gain and loss [exposes General partner's capital to greater downside risk than investors' capital]. (b) 80/20 allocation of all items of income, gain and loss so long as cumulative Fund gains exceed losses; otherwise, allocations made pro rata to capital [permits General Partner's capital to be treated same as investors' capital on downside]. (c) 80/20 allocation of all gain and long-term income; short-term income (i.e., money market interest on idle funds) net of service fee allocated pro rata to capital [Investors may propose this approach on theory that General Partner should not be compensated for making passive, non-venture capital investments]. Investors will want pro rata allocation of net short-term income to be limited (based on fixed number of years or based on percentage of Fund's capital that has gone into venture investments); otherwise, in later years service fees will exceed short-term income, resulting in disproportionate allocation of resulting loss to investors. (d) 80/20 allocation of all gain and long-term income; short-term income, *before* deducting service fee, allocated pro rata to capital [for Investors, pursues same approach

Provision	Summary	Issues
		as (c) above but carries one step further by requiring General Partner to offset 20 percent of service fee against 20 percent "carried" interest].
10. Distributions	The Fund will make cash distributions equal to 30 percent of ordinary income and net realized gains annually, subject to the discretion of the General Partner. The Fund may also make discretionary distributions of cash or securities in advance of liquidation, provided that after giving effect to such distributions, the sum of the net asset value of the Fund plus the amount of all distributions to the Partners equals or exceeds the aggregate capital contributions to the Fund. Any unrealized gain with respect to an in-kind distribution of securities and all other discretionary distributions will generally be made 80 percent to all Partners on the basis of capital contributions and 20 percent to the General Partner.	This area presents the most complex and heavily negotiated issues in venture fund formation, for it deals with the vital question of who gets what, and when. Some of the principal issues are: (a) *Restoration obligation*. Whether, at the end of the Fund, if the General Partner has received more than its "fair share" of distributions (i.e., 20 percent of gain plus pro rata share of balance of gain plus returns of capital), the General Partner must return such excess to the Fund. The General Partner will want to exclude tax distributions, on the theory that these are never received by him. This issue is particularly sensitive for Individual (as opposed to corporate) General Partners, because it may result in personal liability to the Fund. (b) *Escrow of distributions*. Some investors will require that a portion of early distributions to the General Partner be held in escrow to secure any restoration obligations. (c) *Return of capital*. In some cases, the investors must receive all of their capital back from the Fund before any distribution may be made on the 80/20 basis. (d) *Hurdle level*. In this example, the hurdle level (i.e., net assets plus prior distributions divided by total contributed capital) that must be met before discretionary distributions can be made is 1 (i.e., the Fund must have cumulative gains and income greater than losses). In other cases, investors have imposed hurdle levels as high as 1.25, so that gains must equal at least 125 percent of losses. (e) *Valuations*. Because the valuation of Fund investments often plays a critical role in distribution provisions, investors often seek to obtain a role in making such valuations. For example, valuations may be subject to a veto by the Investors; alternatively, the evaluations may require the approval of a Valuation Committee composed of investor representatives. (f) *Mandatory distributions of public securities*. Some investors will seek to require mandatory distributions of all freely traded portfolio securities, arguing that the General Partner is being compensated with its 20 percent carried interest for making private investments, and should not be so compensated for gains resulting from holding publicly traded securities. The General Partner will press for full discretion on these distributions, arguing that the trading market for an emerging company may be adversely affected by the freeing-up of large blocks of stock. Alternatively, the General Partner will argue over the standard for defining "freely traded," particularly whether stock subject to the volume and other limitations of Rule 144 is to be considered "freely traded."

	Provision	Summary	Issues
11.	Service Fee	The Fund will contract with Ad-Venture Management Co., Inc. (the "Service Company") for management, administrative, and clerical services. The Fund will pay to the Service Company an annual service fee equal to 2-1/2 percent of the contributed and committed capital of the Fund.	Issues surrounding service fee arrangements run a close second to distribution issues for amount of scrutiny. Concerns include: (a) *Cost-of-living adjustment ("COLA")*. Whether Fund's fee will increase based on CPI changes. COLAs are disappearing. (b) *Size of fee in relation to size of Fund*. Some Investors will seek to reduce the 2-1/2 percent fee, especially with a larger ($100 million-plus) Fund, where there may be economies of scale, or in later years as Fund winds down. (c) *Size of fee in relation to affiliated Funds*. Where the Individual General Partners are already running earlier venture funds, investors will want assurance that total fees for all of the funds are reasonable in relation to overall costs (economies of scale argument). In addition, many investors will seek to reduce the fee percentage for a Fund's later years, arguing that (i) most of the effort goes into the early years when investments are being made and (ii) by the end of the term of the Fund the Individual General Partners will be organizing a new Fund, which can pay the rent, etc. More recently, some investors have pressed for a cap on cumulative service fees where there is more than one fund. This cap may be tied to total *venture capital* assets under management (rather than total assets, or total committed capital). In other cases, the cap may be tied to total capital but latter figure may be adjusted downward to reflect distributions to partners. (d) *Relation to budgets*. Some Investors will demand that fees be justified on basis of estimated costs (especially salaries and bonuses). Other Investors will demand right, usually exercised via a committee, to approve annual budgets. (e) *Offsets*. Investors may seek to require that any compensation paid to the Individual General Partners by portfolio companies (e.g., directors' fees, stock options, or warrants) be used to offset the fee. The Individual General Partners may resist, pointing out (i) tax complications and (ii) restrictions on transferability, especially with respect to stock options and warrants.
12.	Organizational Expenses	Organizational expenses will be paid by the Fund.	Organizational fees provoke the following issues: (a) *Size*. Almost always subject to a fixed ceiling, usually in $200,000 to $400,000 range (depending primarily on time spent in fund raising and existence of any special issues or complications). (b) *Components*. Items covered, especially where cover salaries, etc. in addition to out-of-pocket costs (travel, printing, legal, etc.)
13.	Conflicts of Interest	The Fund will not invest in portfolio companies of entities affiliated with the Individual General partners. The Individual General Partners may not invest in the securities of any Fund portfolio company.	These are common restrictions. Investors will seek to impose the first restriction to guard against the Fund being used to "bail out" companies in which the Individual General Partners may have an interest. The Individual General Partners will seek an exception for financings with independent third party pricing, such as a requirement that the Fund's investment represent no more than 50 percent of the financing and that the balance be invested by recognized investors with no

Provision	Summary	Issues
		existing interest in the company. The restriction on Individual General Partner co-investing is intended to keep their efforts focused on the Fund.
14. Restrictions and Limitations	The General Partner may not (i) cause the Fund to incur indebtedness or guarantee the obligations of others in an aggregate amount in excess of the Fund's uncommitted holdings of cash and cash equivalents; (ii) organize a successor venture capital fund until the Fund is at least 66-2/3 percent invested; or (iii) amend the Fund's limited partnership agreement without the approval of at least 66-2/3 percent in interest of the limited partners.	Some variations on these points include the following: (a) *Debt/guarantees*. Some investors will seek an outright prohibition; the General Partner may argue for right to incur borrowings or guarantees up to the amount of capital scheduled for contribution to the Fund within the next year. (b) *Successor funds*. Some investors will seek, either as alternative ("later of") or substitute test, a restriction that no successor fund be created for a fixed period (e.g. four years), arguing that investing is only part of the General Partner's job, and that realizing and enhancing gains can be just as time-demanding.

Copyright © 1988 - Testa Hurwitz & Thibeault - 53 State Street - Boston, Massachusetts 02109

Terms for Investing—Part II

Tim E. Bliamptis

The terms used to construct a venture capital limited partnership can dramatically influence the internal rate of return (IRR) received by the limited partners. Some of the effects are obvious, some are less obvious, and some are quite obscure.

Several attributes characterize "good" terms. First, good terms reward the general partner for creating value. Second, good terms create no incentives for the general partner to alter his or her business practices. Third, good terms, though they may be extremely difficult to write, can be understood and implemented in a straightforward manner. Combining all of these characteristics in one document is quite a feat. The law of unintended consequences has a way of insinuating itself into every aspect of a partnership agreement. Terms evolve when unforeseen circumstances require a corresponding change in partnership structures.

The history of venture capital terms clearly illustrates this evolution. One can gain some insight into this process by looking at how the terms change and why they change. In this presentation, I will focus on where terms are going; I will also try to explain why they are changing.

THE EVOLUTION OF TERMS

Table 1 shows the trend in gross returns for the typical partnership started in 1970, 1980, and 1990. These "snapshots" do not correspond to any particular funds; their characteristics are representative of the period. The figures for the 1990 vintage fund are an average of best guesses about what the 1990s will bring.

The recurring theme is change—some cyclical and some monotonic; nothing has stayed the same. Fund size has grown from about $1 million to funds of $100 million and more. Holding periods have ebbed and flowed with the initial public offering (IPO) market. Because of the sensitivity of venture returns to the IPO market, it probably is not surprising that IRRs have also varied widely. The point is that many of the fundamental characteristics of venture partnerships have changed, some by orders of magnitude. An obvious question follows: have terms kept up?

Terms have been evolving, but not as much as one might expect given the tremendous changes in the structure of the industry itself. Table 2 shows four of the most hotly contested terms—terms that have a direct economic impact on the return to the limited partners: carried interest, management fees, capital calls, and distribution policy. Of the four, only carried interest has remained essentially unchanged over time. Although people may argue over the definition of what constitutes profit, the standard carry is and has always been 20 percent. Some firms have commanded premium carries as high as 30 percent, but at least the premium carries are only valuable if the partnership generates profits.

In the 1970s, management fees were based on net asset value (NAV). NAV-based fees are a classic example of a term that creates incentives for the general partner that run contrary to the best interests of the limited partners. There are two parts to the conflict. First, fees are a direct function of valuation: the higher the valuation basis, the higher the fees. This gives the general partner an obvious incentive to write valuations up quickly and to delay writedowns. Second, the general partner earns more current income by delaying distributions. Some partnerships cost themselves and their investors dearly by holding a large amount of distributable securities past the bull market of 1983.

In the 1980s, terms switched to management fees based on committed capital. For funds of modest size, this was a reasonable approach. The problem arose when successful funds began raising ever larger pools of money, while continuing to draw fees from all of the predecessor pools as well. A little quick arithmetic reveals that 2.5 percent of $500 million, for example, is a lot of money; it probably generates a surplus of $8 or $10 million over operation costs. That surplus becomes current income to the general partners. It is safe to say that no other issue has generated as much controversy as the management fee issue—and by no means is the debate over.

It is difficult to predict exactly what will happen. Nonetheless, trends seem to be emerging. In the future, fees will depend on whether a particular fund is a first fund or a follow-on fund, and in what stages the fund will invest. One approach being used

TABLE 1. Trends in Gross Returns

	Multiple	Net IRR	Holding Period	Fund Size
1970	6X	25%	8 yrs.	$ 1 Million
1980	3X	40%	3 yrs.	$ 10 Million
1990	3X	20%	6 yrs.	$ 100 Million

Source: Tim E. Bliamptis and Massachusetts Institute of Technology

increasingly is a fee that varies over the life of the fund. The approach that I prefer, however, is a general partner budget which is reviewed annually by representatives of the limited partners. Certainly, the so-called "plain vanilla" fee will become a thing of the past.

Regarding capital calls, the industry has moved toward drawing its capital as needed. This move was relatively easy to achieve, because once general partners and limited partners were both convinced that slowing capital calls could dramatically increase IRR, changing the term became a "win-win" situation.

Distribution policies have also changed over time, driven by the change of funding sources from individual investors to institutions. Some institutions have been pushing for mandatory distribution of all marketable securities; mandatory distribution may perhaps go too far, but the trend is clearly toward earlier distribution.

TERMS AND THEIR EFFECTS

Terms can be grouped into two categories: those that have a direct effect on IRR and those that have an indirect effect on IRR. I will concentrate on the terms with a direct effect, because they lend themselves to analysis. Those direct effects can be achieved in one of two ways: either by decreasing profits directly, or by changing the timing of the cash flows.

Terms with direct effects on partnership profits include management fees, carried interest, and distribution policies. The annual management fee has an obvious, and, as we shall see, potentially dramatic economic impact on partnership returns. The carried interest term produces economic effects through the profit split mechanism. Unfortunately, the partnership document language can result in different outcomes for two partnerships with supposedly equal carries. Needless to say, it is important to read the documents.

Some terms affect IRRs by changing the timing of the cash flows into and out of the partnership; examples include timing of capital calls, look-backs and other details of how the carry is implemented, and, again, distribution policy. Of these, the timing of capital calls, although the easiest factor to control, can have a tremendous effect on IRRs. The basic rule is "call it when you need it." Although very few partnerships have gone to this extreme, most are now minimizing their idle cash by making smaller, more frequent capital calls.

The relation between terms and return is best illustrated graphically. The assumptions used in Figures 1 through 3 are based on a composite of several highly successful 1979 vintage funds (see Table 3). These assumptions reflect the venture

TABLE 2. Trends in Terms

	1970s	1980s	1990s
Carried Interest	20%	20-30%	20-30%
Management Fees	3% of NAV	2.5% of committed capital	variable
Capital Calls	100% funding	thirds	tenths
Distribution	hold	debate	distribute

Source: Tim E. Bliamptis and Massachusetts Institute of Technology

FIGURE 1. IRR to Limited Partners as a Function of Number of Capital Calls

Source: Tim E. Bliamptis and Massachusetts Institute of Technology

FIGURE 2. IRR to Limited Partners as a Function of Carried Interest

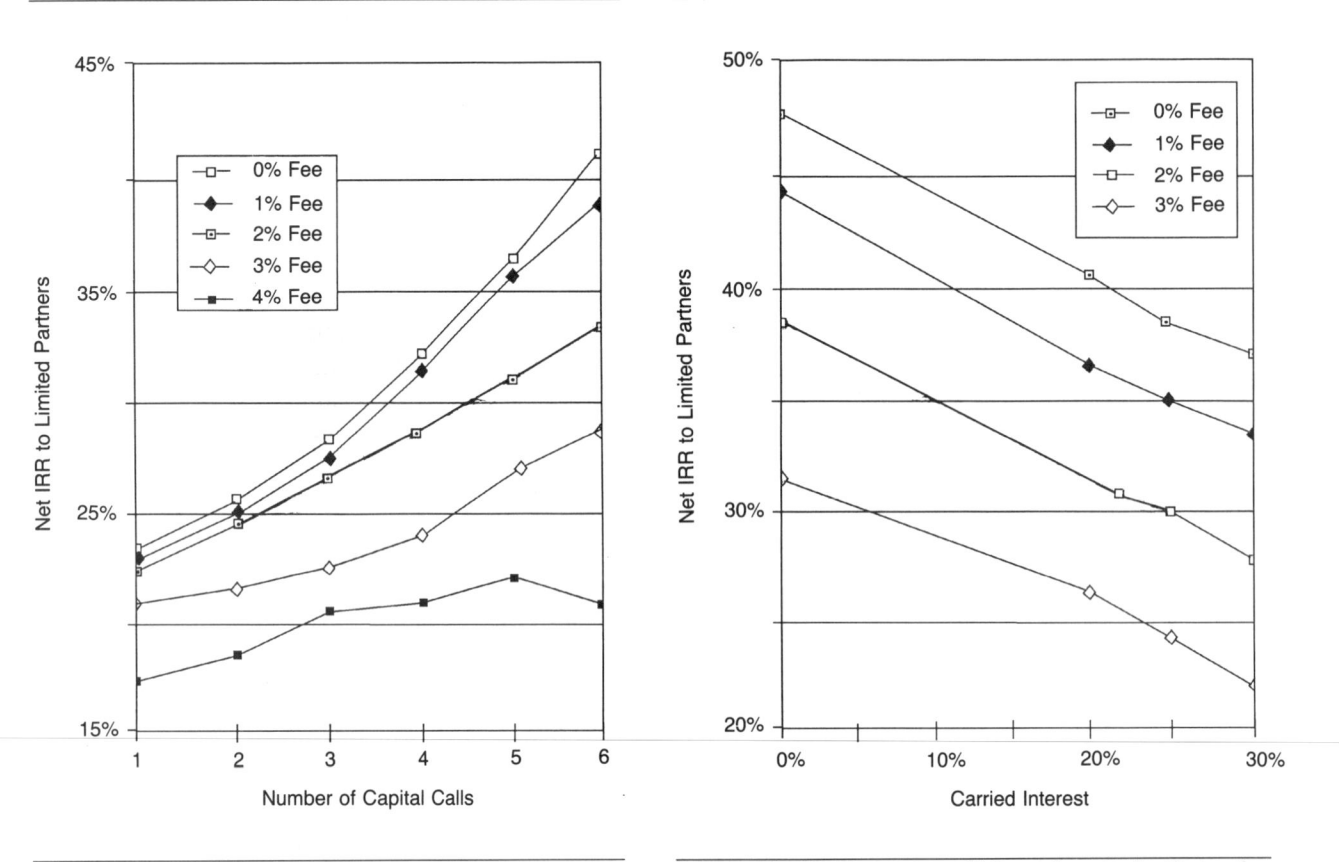

Source: Tim E. Bliamptis and Massachusetts Institute of Technology

capital industry at its peak, but many of the conclusions that flow from them are thus made all the more compelling.

Increasing the number of calls is an easy way to pick up net IRR relative to gross IRR. Figure 1 quantifies this effect, showing the net IRR to limited partners as a function of the number of annual capital calls. The figure shows curves for five different annual fee levels, from zero percent to 4 percent. The curves for 1, 2, and 3 percent fees have steep slopes, indicating that investors can pick up as much as 1,000 basis points just by slowing down the flow of capital. An interesting side effect is that higher fees decrease the benefits of just-in-time funding by "cannibalizing" partnership capital.

The most appropriate term for negotiation between limited partners and general partners is the percentage of carried interest, because a higher carry gives the general partner an appropriate incentive—the general partner benefits only if he generates profits for the limited partners. Moreover, as Figure 2 indicates, increasing the carried interest within the 20 to 30 percent range has a relatively modest effect on IRR.

Figure 2 shows that IRR to the limited partners decreases roughly linearly with increasing carried interest. The relation is shown for three different fee levels, plus a zero fee. The difference in IRR between a 20 percent carry and a 30 percent carry is about 400 basis points—not a lot from the limited partner's point of view, but a tremendous boon to the general partner.

It should be noted that this analysis represents a highly profitable venture fund, where one might expect the carried interest to play a big role. Actually, the economic effect is relatively modest. There is more to the story, however. The analysis assumes some idealized language in the documents—e.g., look-backs and other real-world requirements were not included. Nevertheless, the moral of this story is that given a correctly structured document, the economic effect of changing the percentage carried interest is relatively modest.

Figure 3 shows IRR to the limited partners as a function of annual management fee, with annual fee stated as a percentage of committed capital. The figure shows that it is possible to pick up 500 basis points by cutting the management fee by one

FIGURE 3. IRR to Limited Partners as a Function of Annual Management Fee

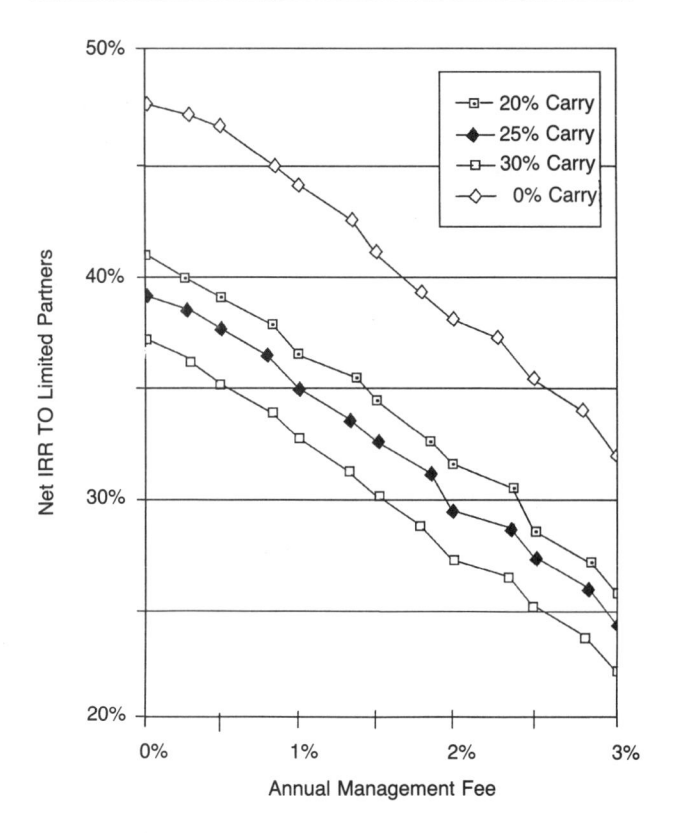

Source: Tim E. Bliamptis and Massachusetts Institute of Technology

percentage point. This indicates that fees are an important determinant of returns to the limited partners. Again, bear in mind that this increase is for an enormously successful fund, where you would not expect fees to have a significant impact.

Does this mean limited partners should mount a campaign to drive down all management fees? Well, not exactly. The size of the management fee should be related to how much money the general partner needs to run his shop. If somebody needs 2.5 percent of committed capital to operate, one should not refuse on the grounds that fees have too great an economic effect. On the other hand, if one is dealing with a large fund where the fees are supporting exorbitant levels of compensation, it might be appropriate to negotiate lower fees.

TERMS WITH INDIRECT EFFECT ON RETURNS

There are also some terms which have indirect effects on the returns to limited partners. Obviously, it is not in the limited partners' best interests to have the general partner starting another business. More specifically, most limited partners do not want the general partner to start another fund until he has fulfilled his obligation to the first. Properly negotiating this term requires walking the line between allowing totally unrestricted behavior and placing onerous limitations on the general partner's activities.

As I mentioned earlier, NAV-based fees have both direct and indirect effects on returns. A NAV-based fee is a terrific incentive never to distribute anything, and to have the most aggressive valuation policies in the business. It makes little sense to base management fees on something which may tempt the general partner to play games.

A distribution policy should allow some room for the general partner to maneuver. If nothing else, the definition of marketable securities should leave enough room so that the general partner is not forced to dump large blocks of stock into thinly traded markets. In addition, some general partners argue that once they have distributed the stock, they lose influence at the board level. This argument is usually based on some variation of the "Just because the IPO is over doesn't mean the venture capitalist's job is over" theme.

I think this is a legitimate argument, although not all institutional limited partners would agree. The problem lies in the need to allow legitimate cases of "more work to do" while preventing abuses. The solution is to eliminate counter-incentives. At the risk of beating a dead horse, consider NAV-based terms again. If the fee is based on net asset value, the limited partner will question the general partner every time he argues that distribution is premature. The goal is to give the general partner the flexibility to run his business without tempting him; a mandatory distribution policy may unnecessarily tie his hands.

Terms that tie fees to committed capital may also tempt general partners. At 2.5 percent of committed capital, a general partner who has raised $400 million

TABLE 3. Assumptions

- Investments return 3.5x in 3 years (52 percent gross IRR)
- Short-term cash returns 5.5 percent
- Net short-term income is distributed annually
- Net short-term income is not available for venture investment

Source: Tim E. Bliamptis and Massachusetts Institute of Technology

over several sequential funds has a $10 million annuity. Venture capital is hard work. Why should the general partners work 70-hour weeks building companies when they can each take home $1 million-plus for doing nothing? As the saying goes, "Why not go to the beach?" I do not suggest that every general partner who has that kind of fee structure has gone to the beach; in fact, far from it. I do, however, suggest that the temptation exists. This creates an incentive which takes the general partner's interests out of sync with the limited partner's interests, and that is the definition of a bad term.

Finally, the terms relating to general partner co-investment rights and limited partner co-investment rights cause the cherry-picking problem—parties somehow related to the general partner try to skim the cream by investing in a handpicked subset of the partnership's deals. Formal co-investment rights give some partners an economic interest which conflicts with the interest of those limited partners who are stuck with all of the investments. Better to allow the general partner the flexibility to syndicate with people who he feels add value. If that includes some of his limited partners, fine.

CONCLUSION

Analysis proves it: terms really do matter. Well-structured terms can improve returns by hundreds or even thousands of basis points. Unfortunately, creating those well-structured terms is not easy, and there is no such thing as one-size-fits-all. Read the documents from a half-dozen recent funds and you will quickly realize that the term "plain vanilla" is misleading. At the very least, there are 10 or 12 recipes out there for it.

The message is: consider all the circumstances. The venture business is too complicated and too sophisticated for a simplistic approach. Every deal is different, and the situation is complicated even further by the fact that the target keeps moving. Terms have been evolving for decades and, if anything, the pace seems to be accelerating.

In this kind of dynamic environment, rules of thumb become suspect. When in doubt go back to the three basic principles: (1) Reward the general partner for creating value, (2) Avoid creating incentives that may alter the general partner's business practices, and (3) Strive for fairness even when you have the upper hand.

Question and Answer Session

QUESTION: Please comment on the market for repurchasing or reselling limited partnership interests.

BLIAMPTIS: The market for secondaries is big and growing. A lot of investors became limited partners in venture partnerships between 1982 and 1984 and, for a variety of reasons, are now trying to sell. I have heard the float in the secondary markets estimated as high as $1 billion. The question is, how does one capitalize on the opportunities? Five years ago it was possible to make phenomenal returns in the secondary markets, but the game is getting tougher. There are a number of intermediaries who tend to conduct auctions which serve the seller more than the buyer. These intermediaries make markets more efficient, and the predictable result is that excess returns are drying up.

QUESTION: Assuming an extended capital call period, what is the risk that a limited partner will renege on its share of the call? Under what conditions is it possible to renege legally?

TESTA: To my knowledge, there have been only two cases of an institution reneging. In both cases, there were very special circumstances. So the history has been very good. The circumstances under which a subscribing limited partner can refuse to pay are extremely limited. For an individual, death is generally the only way to get out of one's obligation. For an institution, the only condition is illegality of the investment. Even then, the refusal to pay must be accompanied by an opinion of counsel confirming that it would be illegal for the institution to go forward. To the best of my knowledge, that clause has never been invoked.

QUESTION: As a limited partner, how does one deal with limited partners who have different opinions about terms?

BLIAMPTIS: Sometimes, the limited partners end up spending as much time negotiating among themselves as they do with the general partner. This situation is quite rare. More often, the limited partners do not talk to each other at all. That is dangerous, because it tempts the general partner to play games, such as telling one limited partner that no one else has ever flagged that term, when in fact other limited partners have voiced concern about it. Communication between limited partners can help alleviate this problem, but ultimately the solution depends on supply and demand; it is a negotiated situation. If there are a lot of buyers and not many sellers, the general partner can control the terms. Certainly, if one buyer is interested in taking a significant percent of the fund, the deal will probably get done on his terms.

QUESTION: What should limited partners do to protect themselves from an overdistribution situation?

TESTA: There are three options. First, delay distributions to the general partner; keep the proceeds technically inside the partnership, so that they remain assets of the partnership available for the restoration obligation. Second, set up an escrow fund for the distribution in kind or cash. Technically, the escrow fund is the property of the general partners, but it is subject to the collateral interest of the fund partnership to get it back. Third, an option which some people think is the least satisfactory, limited partners can require the absolute joint and several obligation of the general partners to pay back prior distributions, if the need should arise.

QUESTION: Is it possible that a fund might never be fully funded?

TESTA: Yes. In fact, recently a long-term technology fund decided that it did not have enough time left in its original stated life of 10 years to meet its target, so it terminated the remaining obligations of the limited partners. The termination was accompanied by the formation of a second fund. Most of the limited partners rolled the extinguished obligation into the second fund.

QUESTION: Doesn't a make-up provision create an incentive for the general partner to distribute less attractive stocks until the make-up provision is fulfilled?

TESTA: In theory, yes. In practice, it is an irrelevant consideration. To the extent that there is distribution in kind of any security, that security must be freely tradeable. Some of the brokerage firms have developed a new business—namely, the instantaneous receipt and sale of securities distributed in kind. This allows fund managers to distribute poor investments to the limited partners by making arrangements with someone who will immediately enter it into a certificate-less system. So, on the date it is received, it is available for sale and you have got good delivery.

QUESTION: Please comment on fees.

TESTA: There are a number of investment advisory firms in this country that offer venture capital advisory services. There are three basic ways of providing the service. First, for a fee, the advisors provide strictly advisory services. The client makes the final decision. Second, the advisors can operate on a totally discretionary basis by informing clients of decisions to invest in various venture capital firms after the fact. A quarterly fee is charged. Third, which is more interesting and will probably become more common, is technically a long-term partnership, which has as its investment objective either investment in other partnerships or occasionally in other partnerships and direct portfolio investments. As the general partner, the advisory firm can charge a straight fee for services or a performance fee.

Current Opportunities and Future Prospects—Part I

Stanley Pratt

The perception that people can earn superior returns in the venture capital industry has attracted many investors in the past 10 years. It is very important to understand that the industry must continue to focus on providing superior long-term returns, rather than on current performance. Venture capitalists are in the returns business, not the investment business. If money is not returned to them, investors will not invest additional monies to start new funds. Unrealized gains are worthless.

Historically, realized returns in the venture industry have been good, averaging 20 to 25 percent. In the next cycle, however, industry average returns will be significantly lower, probably in the 10 to 12 percent range. But industry average returns are not particularly important in inefficient markets. It is quite possible to expect more than the industry average, primarily *because* the market is inefficient. In our opinion, the dispersion of returns earned will be much wider in the future, but it should not be difficult for disciplined analysts to achieve above-average performance.

Because of the inefficient market theory, I disagree with Ms. Marshall's index ideas.[1] I know that if I index in an inefficient market sector, I will get all the turkeys. One can, however, avoid most of the turkeys and get a number of soaring eagles, if one applies careful analysis and disciplines to the partnership selection process.

CURRENT OPPORTUNITIES

The ability to invest capital in private investments has been increased immeasurably by the fact that there are many different ways to invest, including leveraged buyout (LBO) techniques and growth buyouts, as well as in venture capital. People must now focus on their proven skills. I will not invest with venture capitalists if they wanted to start a later-stage fund but only had experience investing in early-stage opportunities, even if they had the best

[1] See Ms. Marshall's presentation, pp. 52-54.

reputation in the country. Kleiner-Perkins, one of the industry's first performers, almost failed with their first fund, which consisted primarily of later-stage investments. In 1974, they made their first early-stage investment—Tandem computers. They followed up Tandem with Genentech and Hybritech. Their earlier investments were later-stage because they were following the crowd, and their track record was miserable. Yet, in later years their return has been one of the finest, because they discovered their strength—early-stage investing—and concentrated on it; they still concentrate on it today.

One of the main trends in the industry today is a return to niche strategies. Investors must have defined strategies. It is not enough just to be opportunistic; strategies must be defined, or investors will be badly hurt. The proper strategy must relate to prior experience. Investors are beginning to understand that the business of building business must be done in a niche. Venture capitalists are moving away from chasing technologies—which are just a way of exploiting a particular application to fulfill a market need. The technologies themselves cannot be exploited.

We look for groups that have clearly defined their niches and understand the barriers to entry in a particular industry. For example, we have quite a few investments in the cable, radio, TV, and paging systems, where there are formidable barriers to entry. Once a company is established in one of those areas, it is difficult for new competitors to enter. We also look for groups that have an unfair advantage through their strategic planning—i.e., good use of strategic partnering. Today, with very short product cycles, when IBM markets a product for a small company, the small company has instant credibility. Strategic partnering will work best when large, established companies market products and services developed by smaller companies. Niche planning in fragmented industries is becoming very popular. If a dominant player in a fragmented industry—for example, funeral homes—can be put together, the rewards may be very high.

Venture investment returns are dependent on

exits. We look for funds that invest in companies that are not totally dependent on going public with an initial public offering (IPO). Recently, we invested in a group that realized a 44 percent per annum return by selling stock back to the management after a seven-year holding period. That can be done in cash flow businesses, because leverage is gained by increasing the company's earnings before interest and taxes (EBIT), and those businesses will always sell within a certain range of an EBIT multiple. LBOs are also being used as an exit technique, by recapitalizing a company after certain objectives have been met. In the past five years, it has really been rather difficult not to make money in the LBO business.

The growth in leveraged buyouts (LBOs) is a plus for the industry. I define venture capital as the business of building businesses; in general, LBOs are the same process. Most LBOs are not in the megadeals like Beatrice Foods or RJR Nabisco. Ninety percent of the LBOs tracked by Venture Economics were smaller than $1 billion purchase price transactions; over half were less than $100 million. LBOs often respond to value added from the venture capitalist, so in many ways they are very close to venture capital and should not be viewed as a separate type of investment.

We often build our portfolios by balancing early-stage partnerships with LBOs. This strategy balances the relatively early return profit characteristics of LBOs with the fact that the early-stage investments do not produce results in the early, developing years.

Asset allocation strategy is extremely important to the venture capital industry. There are important differences between the marketable securities markets, i.e., stocks and bonds, and the nonmarketable venture capital and LBO markets. First, in the stock and bond markets, it is very difficult to obtain above-average performance. In fact, those who do worst are often those who try the hardest to do best. In an efficient marketplace, trying to exceed the average is often a losing strategy; it is often better to buy an index fund. In contrast, private investment offers an opportunity for exceptional returns *because* it is an inefficient marketplace in which the outstanding are able to excel.

Second, the stock and bond markets are very liquid relative to the venture market. Liquidity brings about one of the worst dynamics in our capital structure process: It encourages investors to focus on short-term performance rather than long-term building. In fact, nonmarketable venture capital turns out to have a lot of benefits that people thought were problems in the past. One investor who I trained in the process said to me, "You know, it's very interesting. I now see that a great benefit of venture capital is that it protects me from myself, because in the stock market, when I had a stock in my portfolio that went down for five quarters in a row, either the stock or I left in the sixth quarter. In venture capital, no one knows what's happening. It is wonderful—I could not do anything about it if I wanted to. I have often sold investments that I knew I should hold but was forced to sell because of the emphasis on short-term performance." The dynamics of venture capital provide the opportunity to realize many times the original investment. The lack of liquidity encourages a focus on long-term performance, which will probably increase the overall returns in all capital markets.

RISK-RETURN TRADE-OFF

I would like to debunk one of the industry's most generally accepted myths—that early-stage investing has high risks and high rewards and later-stage investing has lower risks and lower rewards. The risks are different, but not necessarily greater in one or the other. Risk depends on whether investors know how to handle what they are doing. Start-up and early-stage investing have very high business risk, but they generally have low price risk (i.e., overpaying). Later-stage investing and LBOs have a low business risk because the company has existed for some time, and often have a positive cash flow to service the debt needed for an LBO. At this stage, however, the price risk is very high: overpaying for the company will cause a lot of trouble because the time frame for these investments is relatively short. There are some smart LBO people waiting like vultures for overpaid deals to collapse, so that they can pick up the companies at a low price and make some real money. As a matter of fact, in the early-stage and start-up phases, risk can probably be controlled better, because smaller amounts of capital are invested in the early stages; decisions on additional financings depend on whether the company is doing anything right. So, the risk is controlled as the process moves along. In a mezzanine or later-stage investment, or an LBO, 100 percent of the money is invested on the closing day; if the investment is a turkey, there is a real problem.

The return on investments (ROIs) are comparable for the different stages. On a mezzanine or later-stage investment, the return is often 30 to 40 percent per annum for two to three years, whereas early-stage venture capitalists may achieve 20 to 25 percent per annum for seven to ten years. The two are comparable, although they are not the same, because of the effect of time on ROI. The quality is very different, however: I would rather have 20 percent per annum for ten years than 40 percent per annum for five years. Compounding over the longer term produces a lot more money.

CRITERIA FOR A SUCCESSFUL FUND

There are seven criteria for a successful venture capital fund. First, the people must have experience as venture capitalists. I have always called venture capital the last of the apprentice industries: A person is not a good venture capitalist until we can count his or her battle scars. This business must be learned from the bottom up. Anyone who has not lost a company and not fired friends is not a venture capitalist.

Second, it is extremely important that everyone in a venture capital partnership work together as a team. We have seen funds in which the general partners got together solely for marketing purposes. On paper, it looked like they would be able to raise money, but once they got going, the partners discovered that they hated each other; those are not the kind of people that I want investing my money. For this reason, we invest only in partnerships that have already demonstrated that they can work well together.

Third, the people should have special skills and industry experience.

Fourth, judgment capabilities are extremely important. Individual funds have their own decision processes. Therefore, it is important to determine whether the process the fund has adopted will work for its personnel and its strategy. For example, I recently analyzed two funds whose decision processes were totally opposite. In my opinion, however, each company used the process that was right for itself. Had either tried to use the other's system, it would have failed. The companies had built systems around particular individuals that would work only for those personnel. For this reason, it is important to look very hard into what is going on within funds.

Another judgment capability is to determine the optimal exit time. There is a propensity for most venture capitalists to stay with their disappointments too long, especially when raising money every two or three years. Venture capitalists hate write-offs; they want to defer them as long as possible. They must be able to recognize when to get out of an investment so that something is still salvageable. It is also necessary to be able to judge when to stay with those investments that, with the proper shepherding, will be profitable. In general, venture capitalists stay too long, partly because of their egos and partly because they are involved in too many things.

FIGURE 1. Venture Capital Performance

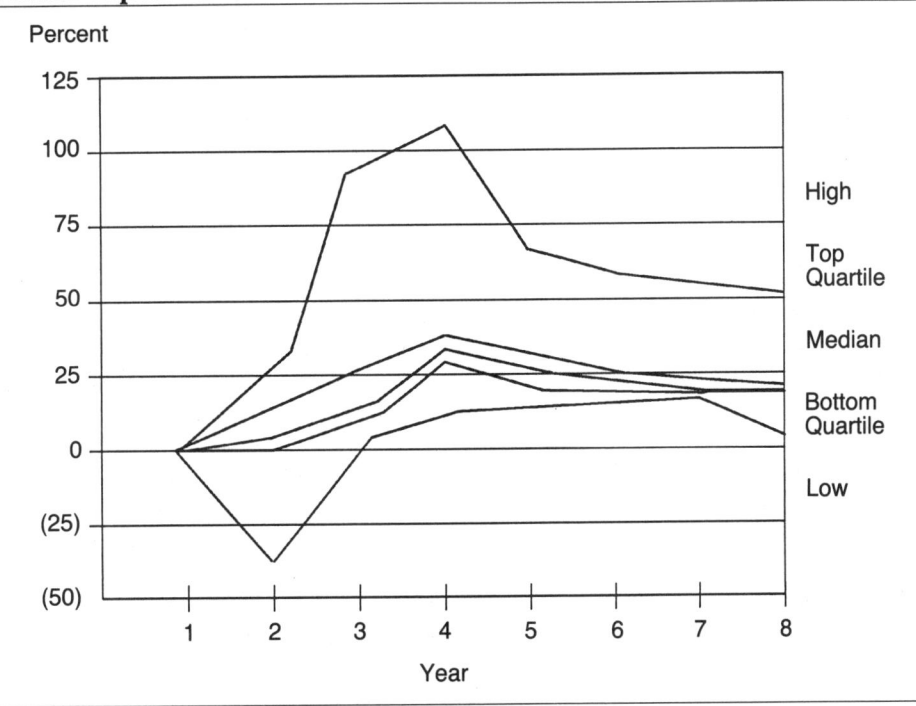

Source: Venture Economics

The fifth criteria is rate of return. Figure 1 shows the dispersion of returns of a group of venture capital funds formed in the same year. Even after the very misleading early indications had settled down, the recorded internal rates of return (IRRs) after seven years (when much of the capital had been distributed to the investors) ranged from 52 percent per annum to 21 percent in the top quartile and from 14 percent to 4 percent in the bottom quartile. The professional manager's job is to create portfolios that perform much better than the averages. To do this, it is more important to avoid the bad ones than to find the specific high fliers. If all we do is avoid the ones that drag the average down, we will do better than the average. By averaging everything, all the wealth of information is hidden. In my opinion, 1983 was the single most destructive year to the venture capital process in the 25 years that I have followed it, because it brought about unrealistic expectations and made people think they were doing things that they really were not doing at all.

The last two criteria are the characteristics of the fund's portfolio of investments and the personalities and personal chemistry of the people involved.

EVOLVING OPPORTUNITIES

Two trends in the venture industry are very important: the trend toward corporate partnering and the trend toward international activities. Corporate strategic partnering is just beginning. Both large corporations and venture capitalists are still learning how to use each other. This new tool can be extremely effective, primarily when the corporation provides more than money. The relation can also be less than satisfactory. Venture capitalists will be disappointed when they go to a corporation for the sole purpose of getting a high price for a financing so that they can mark up their old stock to help raise money. Generally, the corporate partners never really put a specific price on the stock; they combine into one sum the value of a technology or a marketing agreement, and the purchase of stock. Venture capitalists only look at the money paid and the number of shares sold, without taking the other factors into account. They mark stocks up to that price as an unaffiliated round of financing, and then get into real problems. Some companies have been hurt by the venture capitalists' reluctance to let them go public for less than what they marked their stock up to. For example, Sun Microsystems was delayed in going public by one year because the venture capitalists based the minimum price on the amount that Kodak paid, but Kodak had purposely combined the stock and all the agreements into one transaction, and Kodak's payment had little relation with the price of the stock. Sun Microsystems had to wait until it could be brought public above the false price. Corporations that know how to work with venture capital companies and small portfolio companies can provide a tremendous amount of potential value added.

International activities—global markets and technology transfer—are an extremely important part of venture capital. The international activities have a larger effect in buyout areas than in other spheres of venture. Every company in the world with positive cash flow is a target for a buyout, whereas technology-oriented venture capital, as is practiced in the United States, can work in very few other infrastructures. For example, it has been very difficult to get companies in the Pacific Rim out of the hands of the few families who control much of many nation's assets. Often, these owners would gladly get rid of some of these investments to realize liquidity and make money, but they cannot do so because they do not know how.

The LBO process will be extremely important in realigning the capital markets in many foreign countries. This process has already happened in the United Kingdom. For example, LBOs provided a major impetus for the development of the U.K. venture capital market. When I first tried to develop the British venture capital process, there were many problems. One of the biggest hurdles was the British people's reluctance to break with establishment to start a new business. For this reason, it was difficult to develop entrepreneurship there; we only succeeded when entrepreneurs who had been running divisions of poorly managed companies emerged to buy the divisions. Managers were suddenly able to buy companies that had been run solely to generate dividend income for the shareholders, who happened to be members of the founding families. They often found that they could run the company much better when they did not have to make dividend payments. We think this process was extremely important in the United Kingdom, and that it will be pivotal in many other parts of the world.

FUTURE TRENDS

In the future, I believe that realized returns will be much more widely dispersed as a result of inefficient markets, which enable the outstanding to excel and the mediocre to fail. Many more venture capital funds will fail than excel. An industry could never grow the way venture capital has without bringing in some people who are not as good as other people. The expectation that all venture capitalists could be great was unrealistic. The fact is, if venture capital were easy, we would not need venture capitalists.

The debate will continue about whether large funds can add more value than small funds. Recent data indicates that larger funds have performed better, but almost exclusively for the reason that the only people who can raise large funds are the most experienced venture capitalists. Historically, all seed money came from families. Seed funds did not begin to form until the early 1980s, and there has not been enough time for many of them to prove themselves. Many people made mistakes with early seed funds. For example, if a standard venture capital fund has a 10- to 12-year life, a seed fund ought to have a 12- to 15-year life, but many seed funds were formed with a 7-year life. The bottom line is that some venture capital partnerships will prosper, and some will not. It is incumbent upon investors to determine which funds are likely to succeed in the future.

PERFORMANCE MEASUREMENT

For venture capital, performance measurement requires much greater depth than for conventional investments. According to a Venture Economics returns study, interim performance indicators are almost always misleading. Interestingly enough, performance patterns are not generally the traditionally accepted J-curves, but often are sine waves. This is because of 1983, when everything looked great for a while before turning downward; with any luck, it will look better again toward the end of the partnership.

It is important to look at the quality of the actual returns. Were they a result of skill or luck? Are they consistent? There are many ways of realizing the returns. For example, in some cases it is possible to get an 8 to 9 percent cash-on-cash return and later enough capital gains to provide a 20 to 25 percent per annum return on a mezzanine fund. Currently, we are considering investing in a buyout-type fund that has returned over 30 percent per annum for the past seven years; much of the return has been cash.

It is also important to evaluate strategies, disciplines, and aggregate portfolio analysis. I can examine 65 partnerships on my desktop computer. Although we are able to compare these funds to see how they are being valued, it is not worth my management time to think about it. The individual valuations are not really very different, and deviations are almost always cured in the next quarter.

CONCLUSION

The venture capital industry needs its own specialists who have unique expertise in the industry: They must be dedicated to investment performance; exercise due diligence as a principal; and have the experience and judgement to predict performance over the next decade. They must have fiduciary responsibility with accountability. The professional's responsibility must be clearly defined, the commitment must be long enough to extend over job cycles, and conflicts of interest must be eliminated. That is what the industry needs to be orderly in the future.

I am shocked by the lack of due diligence by some of the institutional investors. Some investors simply do not want to take the time to research funds thoroughly. Investment managers specializing in venture capital do not perform due diligence as an agent. Because we have fiduciary responsibility, we perform due diligence as a principal: I must protect myself, not my client. It is extremely important that we do an enormous amount of due diligence prior to every investment commitment.

In conclusion, I think that venture capital partnerships with highly skilled managers will be a very prudent vehicle for diversification and will provide very satisfactory relative returns in the future. It is very important, however, to be selective. Discipline is vital, and it is something we lacked in the early 1980s.

Current Opportunities and Future Prospects—Part II

Rodney H. Adams

Over the past five years, there have been dramatic and significant changes in the venture capital industry. To a large measure, these changes have been negative. Both the economics and the demographics are quite different today than they were throughout most of the history of venture capital. The current era of venture capital originated in approximately 1946 when General Doriot founded American Research and Development Corporation. I say the current era, because some people observe that the American railroad industry was financed by venture capitalists in the early 1800s—in this case, Scottish investors. Today, with the strong interest in venture capital, it is hard to believe that in 1974 *Institutional Investor* published a cover story that asked the question, "Is venture capital dead?"[1] While it may be hard to believe today, there was a time 15 years ago when about 12 to 18 months elapsed with virtually no IPOs, and again venture capitalists thought the whole game was over. In that sense, the 1973-74 market crash in the IPO market was worse than the October 1987 stock market crash, in that everyone just left the industry hanging.

TRENDS IN SUPPLY AND FEES

Because of the increased interest in venture capital returns, the amount of money committed to this area has skyrocketed. In addition, the amount of money under management, but not yet invested, has also risen dramatically. There is a lot of cash waiting to be invested in new ventures. The problem is finding attractive investments. Unfortunately, there are some people who are impatient—because their investors do not want idle cash—and who are trying to find companies in which to invest as soon as the money comes in. That may be a very small sample, but the trend is disturbing. In this industry, it may not be a mistake to go for a year or two without making an investment. Some venture funds have gone long periods without making investments, and then, all of the sudden, make a number of investments in one quarter because things have turned around. Investors should not harass general partners about getting the money out.

Another trend shows that the amount of money needed to fund a new venture has increased at a slower rate than the money available. More money is migrating toward later-stage and mezzanine-stage funding and, of course, into some leveraged buyouts (LBOs). The amount of money that is going into the earlier stages—seed, start-up, and first round—appears to be declining. This trend has important implications for the industry. Stanford University as a limited partner has moved toward early-stage investing, although we were never extensively involved in later-stage investing. This is a somewhat contrarian approach, but we think it is the one that has the potential for adding the most value to the process.

The trend in the number of venture firms is decidedly on the upswing. The number of venture firms has increased significantly, doubling over the past five years. Over the past 10 years, there has been a five-fold increase. The growth in the number of funds has brought a significant increase in the number of people entering and involved with the business. Most venture capitalists now have less than five years experience. Venture capital partnership documents should be examined to determine how much experience the individuals have.

Fee schedules are also changing. In the early days, management fees were actually just an expense item, a budget control item; they were not a percentage of anything. Today, three or four venture capital fund partnerships still operate that way! The purpose of these fees is to cover costs, not to provide compensation. Ten years ago, fees were calculated using a net-appraised-value approach, which seemed to make sense at the time. Unfortunately, it did not work because it resulted in limited partners being on the other side of the tracks from the general partners over the valuation of the portfolio. Next, the industry moved to a percentage of committed capital. The discussion now centers on whether all

[1] "Venture Capital's Great Identity Crisis," *Institutional Investor*, July 1974.

sequential partnerships in a fund group should receive the same percentage. Mr. Bliamptis argued that the fee should be a function of the size of the fund, what they are doing, and, most importantly, whether it is a family of partnerships.[2] On a $35-million fund that is doing seed investing, a fee of 2.5 to 3.5 percent may be reasonable to cover expenses. Conversely, on a $50-million megapartnership in a fund group, a fee of 2 percent on each partnership is unconscionable; the fee must be calculated differently.

The people who are most responsible for the high fees are the limited partners who do not do their due diligence. In one case, we tried very hard to get a general partner to agree to a lower management fee. Before he agreed, he made calls to two major corporate pension funds. In both corporations, the analysts offered to invest without questioning the terms. Needless to say, the general partner elected to get money from the limited partners who accepted their fee; they had no reason to accept our terms.

One of the big changes in the industry is the advent of megafunds: Now, the idea of creating $100-million funds no longer brings shudders to investors. Similarly, the trend has been toward larger investments in individual companies. The first two or three rounds of funding of a company, however, are still quite often less than $10 million. The amount of money that is going into the venture business has gone up 10 to 20 times, but the amount of money actually invested in companies has gone up only two to three times. A discrepancy still exists.

PROBLEMS WITH SUPPLY/DEMAND IMBALANCES

The balance between supply and demand is cause for concern. The growing number of venture partnerships and the amount of money available for investment, combined with about the same number of good deals, has changed the dynamic. In the past, there was much heavier networking and much more sharing of deals. Competition to get the deal could be intense, but once there was a handshake, the deal was done. There was some sharing and some syndication. Recently, it appears that even after a deal is agreed upon, some venture firms will offer more money in an attempt to convince the management to renege on a handshake agreement. This practice is quite disturbing. A secondary effect of this practice is that information about deals is not shared as much, unless the people can really be

[2]See Mr. Bliamptis' presentation, pp. 64-68.

trusted. There has been a closing of the ranks, in that the network of people that venture capital general partners converse with has shrunk. This is unfortunate because it is vital to have a network of trusted partners who can provide additional insights or a different perspective on venture investments.

Another problem with the large amount of cash available is that venture capitalists are tempted to invest in companies that look good and then leave them alone. Most investments require additional work. There is more to venture capital than just writing checks and then driving down the road to the next company to see if they will take a check. This approach does not add much value.

TRENDS IN PERFORMANCE EXPECTATIONS

There is a trend in the industry to enhance performance reporting. Some investors want funds to report both the best and the worst results. I am sure this is prompted by some limited partner investors who must report results, either to their superiors or to their clients.

Because of the changing dynamics in the industry, performance in the next decade, in my opinion, will be bimodal. For most people, returns will be significantly below prior experience and recent expectations. On the other hand, some will earn higher returns. For the most part, the higher returns will accrue to people investing in deals in which the venture capitalist is creating tremendous value and dealing in a market that is truly inefficient, one in which they can seize a comparative advantage. There will be a big difference, and before putting money into partnerships, it is important to think about the disparity.

Venture capital investor performance should be considered in cohorts. The most important breakdown is time cohorts. The performance of a venture partnership that is three years old cannot be equated with one that is five or ten years old; the two are quite different. One of our trustees swears that I have lost my touch: I picked very good venture capitalists in the 1960s and 1970s, but terrible ones in the late 1980s. Yet, I have picked exactly the same people and the same funds! The trustee does not understand the changing dynamics. Recent performance has been affected by the J-curve of the industry, the capital markets, and the cyclical nature of venture capital investing. Earlier, I noted that some thought venture capital looked dead in 1973 and 1974. We are going through a similar cycle now, and I believe that future returns probably will be lower, although current returns will come back somewhat from their current lows. In the 1990s, returns to limited partners may be in the high teens.

The 1983-87 cycle is like a boa constrictor that swallowed a huge animal: The animal must be digested, and finally work its way out in a five-year, seven-year, or ten-year set of returns. In 1982 and 1983, competition was intense for many deals. Many venture capital funds broke their discipline and paid too much for companies. That was the marketplace: There was a booming initial public offering (IPO) market, so people paid higher prices. But the October crash destroyed the IPO market. The net effect is that companies going public in the next few years will probably do so at lower valuations than they would have four or five years ago. Also, because the IPO market is not as vital right now, it will take a year or two longer for companies to go public. Lower returns result when delayed a year or two in going public, and this will cause the IRR to come down. Once this information is digested, the prospects will be brighter.

One trend that scares me is the amount of money flowing *out* of the business. Years ago, if people wanted to sell secondary positions in limited-partner interests, the other limited partners had a preferential right. The process was random, and there were at the most two or three a year. Now, I get at least two letters a month from different intermediaries, providing lists of all of the limited partnership interests that are available on the secondary market. The message is that people are getting out. I am afraid that as the present lower returns become more publicized, more people may try to get out. In fact, many institutional investors can be criticized for their tendency to push a lot of money into a market and then pull it out.

In contrast to many people, we believe that the megafunds as a group (with exceptions) will produce a lower total return to the investors than the small, old-style fund groups that get involved with their companies. The Venture Economics data indicate that it is the other way around—that the very large funds have done better.[3]

INTERGENERATIONAL TRANSFERENCE

In my opinion, one key to success in the future is investing with known good funds—name funds. This is a people business. In his presentation, Kevin Landry listed several criteria for investing, but he forgot that the real key to investing is that the first decision is management, the second one is management, and the third one is management.[4] After that, one worries about the market. The name of a fund group tends to have much more momentum than some of the individual general partners involved in that group. This is not true in all cases, but it does hold true for a number of them. Concentrating strictly on past performance of a fund group may obscure the fact that the people who actually made those decisions and who were responsible for that performance are now no longer active general partners; although they may still be special limited partners. It is a whole new game, because the people have changed. People matter as much as selecting the companies in choosing venture capital partnerships. Investors must ask who makes the decisions in a fund group. I am very critical of limited partners who have not done the due diligence to find out whether the key names of an established name group are still active.

One of the biggest issues that must be faced in the 1990s is "intergenerational transference." The people who have created a tremendous name for themselves and have been very successful cannot live forever. Decision-making responsibility must be transferred to the next generation. There are now three generations in venture capital. The first generation consists of people that have been in the business for 25 or 30 years; the second group has been investing for about 10 years; and the third group for five years or less. Evidence of that transfer is apparent. Some fund groups transfer extremely well, but others do not. In trying to pick a venture capital partnership, the signals are sometimes intuitive. For example, when four or five general partners come to a meeting and only one person does all the talking, I assume that this person makes all the decisions. My impression of these partnerships is not favorable. This sort of thing does not appear in the documentation, but it is clearly something that must be considered.

Venture capitalists must be in close contact with companies to get a sense of management's effectiveness. A venture capitalist who is involved in the creation of the company will probably be forced to fire an entrepreneur who has become a good friend, because it is very rare to find an entrepreneur who is a good manager; more often than not, professional management must be brought in. Firing someone is a very hard thing to do: It is probably the most unpleasant part of a venture capitalist's job, but it is necessary. It is part of the reason venture capitalists deserve the pay that they

[3]See Ms. Vincent's presentation, pp. 26-30.

[4]See Mr. Landry's presentation, pp. 32-38.

get.

The form of remuneration has a strong impact on incentives. A few venture capitalists have no taxable income; their return is all capital gain. Those people have the most incentive to perform. Not only are their interests parallel with those of limited partners, but their whole concept of remuneration is to make gains for both themselves and investors. In the past, most of them received modest incomes. In recent years, however, there have been cases where income levels are very high. In these instances, we ask, what are the incentives? What are the goals?

I am not sure how investors should get started. One option is to use a fund of funds. Another way is to use consultants; they do not invest your money, but give advice. Eventually, with experience, it is possible to make decisions about partnerships. To go beyond that into direct investing is treacherous. Only unusual institutional investors can make successful direct investments into companies. Direct investing requires being involved in almost every aspect of growing a business, not just providing money. I cannot see how it is possible to do that and run a pension fund or an endowment.

CHARACTERISTICS OF A GOOD VENTURE PARTNERSHIP

In my opinion, there are six characteristics of all good venture partnerships. The first is an excellent "practice of partnership," which means that all of the principals work together closely in making critical investment decisions. If one guy does all the talking, it is not a partnership. One practice sheds light on the dynamics of a partnership. Some very well-managed fund groups have a matrix of how many directorships each partner is on, when each partner joined the board, and when they must resign to serve on another company's board. These firms are managing that process; they are practicing their profession in a prudent, controlled way.

A second element of a successful venture partnership is whether the funding is adequate. Adequate funding cannot be broadly defined: It is a very personalized question. Important considerations are the amount of money the firm puts out each year, the amount put out each year per partner, and whether that rate can be sustained. If there is too much capital in the partnership—perhaps because partners' egos are driving them to obtain a much higher amount of money—there may be problems because they may not have the personnel, ability, or time to invest that money properly. On the other hand, if there is not enough money, the partners will not be able to get adequate participation in deals.

A third major criterion is original deal flow. This includes all aspects of creating deals. Caution must be used, however, in talking with venture capital general partners about definitions of terms, such as "lead investor." I have yet to meet a venture capital general partner who is not a lead investor. But then the question arises of how many of their companies' boards do they serve on. It is not possible to accept what is written; due diligence is required.

Fourth, I think it is important to invest a significant portion of a fund in early-stage investments—at the seed- or first-round stage.

Fifth, the equity participants should be involved in their companies. They should be on the board of most portfolio companies, and build value through "sweat equity." In fact, they should not make investments in companies that are so far away that they cannot be monitored.

The final criterion for successful venture capital investing is a focused, consistent application of partners' strengths. We do not invest in focused partnerships—those which invest only in communications, for example. We know that many limited partners believe that there must be a focus, but we have found that over the past 20 years, the more successful venture capital partnerships have followed the cycle and have been later-stage at some points for a larger portion of their portfolio, earlier-stage at other points. The key is that these partnerships have always gone with their strengths. If they have no experience in biotech, they might spend several years gaining strength before betting on that industry. They have gone with their strengths, but they have also been opportunistic. It is far better to watch strengths change than bet that for the next 10 years a certain industry will be successful. I cannot make that bet, and I will not give money to anyone who thinks he can.

Panel Question and Answer Session

VINCENT: I think commitment levels in 1988 will be the same as or somewhat below 1987. Commitments in the first half of 1988 were exactly the same as the amount of money raised by private independent venture funds in the first half of 1987. For the past few years, the second half of the year has been much bigger, so we would expect that more money would come in. There is a difference between the private independent venture groups, which are raising other people's money, and financial captive corporate groups, or corporate development operations, in which the parent company's money is invested. About 25 percent of the funds comes from those captive groups. This number is driven by who is in the marketplace at any particular time. In 1988, we had fewer megafunds raised than in the previous year so its possible we'll see a decline in new commitments.

QUESTION: What type of investor should invest in first funds?

SWENSEN: Not all first funds are alike. If a first fund has people with diverse experiences—for example, a person from the financial community, a person who has done turnarounds, a person who knows industry well, and a person who has spent some time in a venture capital partnership—that partnership may be considered. Investors must do their due diligence before deciding whether to invest in first funds. We avoid investing in first funds when they have not operated as a partnership prior to raising the money. It is very important that a partnership has a track record and has been tested to ensure that partners are able to work together. We almost broke that rule about two or three months ago: We were about to recommend an investment to our investment committee, when an article in the *Wall Street Journal* said that the partnership had exploded.

ADAMS: I preface my answer by saying that we have violated every rule in the book regarding venture. We have invested in some first funds: We feel that it is a mistake to have a blanket prohibition against it, although some institutions have such a prohibition. We bet on people. For example, we invested in one entity that would be considered a first fund by many people. It was a group of people who actually had working experience, but only with family money. For the first time, they were going after institutions, but nobody would touch them because they had not been out before. But they had a lot of experience. In our assessment, they are probably one of a large group of really successful next-generation funds, so we invested with them. We also put money with a man who had been in the investment business, had successfully managed a biotech company, and now wanted to combine the two and create a small fund including two other people as partners. Investing in first funds is very tricky, but it should not be ruled out.

QUESTION: There is some controversy about whether large funds, by virtue of their size, will be able to perform at the same level as small funds. As funds grow in size, should potential limited partners consider not only the past performance and the people but also how the organizational structure is changing to take advantage of the new asset size being managed?

VINCENT: Present data suggests that of the groups that formed funds in the early 1980s, the larger funds are doing somewhat better after four years of operation. It would be necessary, however, to look at each individual fund to determine what is causing better performance. As I stressed before, it is important to know how much of that IRR number has actually been distributed. Because of the changing dynamics in our industry and the large amount of capital under management, people are looking at LBO deals to give a kick to the IRR, but this may not, in the long run, be sustainable. I will be very interested in the internal rate of return when these funds are liquidated. I think historical precedent suggests that the smaller, early-stage focused funds stand a chance of outperforming other groups later in their life.

ADAMS: I am a proponent of putting money into small funds, very early-stage, but there are anomalies. In general, I think that large megafunds get a little too financial, a little too syndicated-oriented, but there are exceptions. There is one large megafund group that has its own patented approach to getting really good deal flow. You have to participate in this one, even though their fees are quite high, because it will be successful.

BLIAMPTIS: To examine the return question a little bit, consider the 1974 vintage Kleiner-Perkins partnership. They did about 15 deals, three of which were 100-times winners: Hibertech, Genentech, and Tandem Computer. That is a small fund—no big fund will ever produce that kind of a result. The chance of getting more than one 100-times winner in a portfolio is very small, even if you have 50 or 60 companies in a portfolio. The way the business has gone, I do not think there will ever be that level of preposterously successful results again. If it does happen, it will be a small fund.

SWENSEN: Size may, in some way, reduce a fund's ability to generate returns, but the relation between size and performance may be influenced by other effects. For example, it could be that larger funds are raised by established groups with a track record. For this reason, high-quality groups with good performance are able to raise more money, gaining the inverse relationship between size and returns.

JOHNSON: I would add that the bigger funds can attract more people and pay pretty good salaries because they get a lot of money from the management fee. I prefer medium-sized funds, but the key to success is people. Very strong groups that can do good deals attract a lot of money. With the same talent, a small fund should be able to outperform a big fund.

QUESTION: What is causing people to stay away from early-stage deals?

JOHNSON: I have a fundamental belief that the starting of new companies is needed in our capitalistic society. The fundamental act of creating a new company—finding a marketplace, finding people, raising money, using the talent and energy of the venture capital company—creates value if the company is successful. The amount of value created will depend on the stock market, correct estimates of market size, and many other things. But fundamentally, it is a profit-producing act. I would say that there are some risks about success, but not a lot of risk about valuation: For $100-million companies, which most people are trying to start, after the first couple of rounds the valuations with the new money still stay down in the $10 to $20 million range.

ADAMS: I believe that the trend away from early-stage deals has happened because the later stage is safe, secure, and less risky. It is a delayed effect of the October 19, 1987 crash—people reacted in ways that they may not even be able to articulate themselves. There are a small number of very experienced venture capitalists doing business as usual in the smaller companies: They are not afraid; they have not run for cover. A number of people in the industry have become afraid, and it makes me question their commitment to the venture business. This is not the first time people have become worried. For a number of years after the *Institutional Investor* article, "Venture Capital's Great Identity Crisis", only a very small number of firms would fund a new company. In the early 1980s, everyone wanted to fund start-up deals. There have been extremes on both ends, and we are seeing an extreme now.

JOHNSON: Money is made in entrepreneurship not by going directly after money, but by creating companies that have terrific research, have terrific products, are going after a large market, and build strong organizations. Investing in later rounds does not really contribute much to that process. The goal is to guess the valuation the public market while carrying out a financial transaction. The excitement and the value come from concentrating on the business issues; the money is a by-product of successful business operations.

QUESTION: Given the dynamism of the economy in regions of the country other than California and Massachusetts, as well as the appearance of skilled venture capital managers in these regions, why don't Stanford, MIT, and Yale invest aggressively in some of these newer areas where there are good deals, less competition, and local venture capitalists to seize them?

ADAMS: In the past, we invested in various geographic regions: We almost had our head handed to us in the process, which may be the reason we do not do it now. Prior to making an investment, we look at the area of investment, the infrastructure, and whether that region could sustain entrepreneurial activity and new company formation. For example, if a company needs 25 people who are good at soldering printed circuit boards, it would be easy to find them in Sunnyvale, California but much harder in the middle of Iowa. We invest in areas of the country that are growing and attractive, not for diversification's sake. We recently made a commitment in the Rocky Mountain area because we believe that area is attractive. We rejected the same commitment five years ago, because we did not think the region could support the project. We have put money in Japan, another area of venture capital that is fertile. Thus, we have provided ourselves with a little bit of geographic diversification.

BLIAMPTIS: I would add that if you are attached to a particular area, you had better be right. No one would want to raise a fund to invest in the Bermuda Triangle: Once you are there you cannot get out. A national-based fund has more options; if things dry up in one region, they can go somewhere else.

SWENSEN: Like Stanford, Yale has diversified the venture portfolio internationally. We feel that we are not smart enough to identify those regions where the deals are going to be best, so we invest in firms we are confident will be able to find the best deals, regardless of where they are located.

QUESTION: It seems that the consensus view is that returns will be lower in the future. If the expected rate of return is lowered to between 15 and 20 percent, does it make any difference?

ADAMS: No. The absolute rate of return does not make a difference to us, provided that whatever the return is, it is higher than the alternatives. Although returns are expected to be down, the alternatives are almost always in a lower-expected-return vehicle. It will be interesting to see what happens to those investors who decided to jump in because they hoped for a 30-percent return and who will bail out because it is now 20 percent.

VINCENT: The most important thing to note is that the expected return for the venture industry is an average. By definition, there are some numbers that are considerably higher, and some that are considerably lower. Not everyone will earn 20 percent. The portfolio that Mr. French illustrated was an indication of the kinds of results that may be achieved when professionals do the level of work that is required to pick the best funds.[1] I am not saying that the investors in this room are not going to make mistakes: Some picks will be below the average. But the numbers suggest that we have to pay a lot more attention to the due-diligence process, and we have to spend the time that this very labor-intensive asset class requires.

BLIAMPTIS: We must remember that university endowments represent the longest time horizon investors: For university endowments, the time horizon is infinite, relative to just about anyone else's—we have the luxury of 10 to 20 years. In addition, we have the luxury of trustees who are on board for a long time, and understand both the institution's needs and the way the venture capital business works. I cannot speak for my colleagues, but I do not take a lot of heat if quarterly numbers are down. Those investors who do take the heat must think about different issues than we do. Venture capital is a perfect asset class for us, but it might not be for other investors.

SWENSEN: I am not sure that expected returns will be 15 to 20 percent. Some leading venture capital groups indicate that returns for the industry as a whole might be as low as 10 percent. I think there is also an expectation of greater variation in returns among groups, so the dispersion will be much larger. If I believed that we would to be earning 10 percent on venture, I do not think we would have much of a commitment, if any. But I think we are in a position to select superior groups, avoid inferior groups, and, therefore, end up meeting our target return, which is about 20 percent. I believe that there will be a lot of disappointment going forward, even if people are expecting 15 to 20 percent returns.

JOHNSON: The low returns that investors are currently earning are not necessarily the returns that will be gained in the future. I think the returns on new funds will average in the teens and the spread around it probably will range from 10 to 30 percent, with extreme performers beyond that.

SWENSEN: One of the reasons there is a difference of opinion regarding future returns is that the question remains unanswered as to whether we are in the bottom part of a cycle and things are going to turn back up, or whether there was a structural change in the industry in the early 1980s. I think that the huge increase in funds may have caused some sort of structural shift that will take a long time to work out. There will be partnerships that continue to do well and survive through this difficult time, but the industry as a whole will have problems because of the amount of money that has been raised.

QUESTION: What items have you changed in partnership subscription agreements, and what changes did you ask for?

PRATT: One of our main concerns is management fees. We want to have management fees integrated among the different funds under management. We do not mind spending money when it is spent wisely; we do not like our fees to be divided up at the end of the year to provide enormous bonuses to a few

---

[1] See Mr. French's presentation, pp. 23-25.

general partners.

We feel very strongly that there must be look-backs. That is, if for some reason the general partners get more than the 20 percent profit interest that they are supposed to get—which can happen in the complexity of partnership allocations—we want at least a partial look-back to right ourselves. Obviously, we invest in people, and if the partners tell us they will give a look-back, we tell the lawyer to write it up, but it does not have to be tightly locked up through escrow.

We are also interested in the vesting of the general partners' interest. We have turned down a number of partnerships for one simple reason: the sponsoring institution kept too much of the carry for itself. We feel that the people who are out there knocking themselves out should get the carried interest, not the sponsoring institutions. We do not want the people who were there for the raising of the fund to get all of the general-partner carry in perpetuity; we want them vested over at least five years, or preferably the length of the partnership. We are astounded to find that general partners are rarely asked questions about vesting. They are seldom asked how much they are paid, and they often do not want to answer that question. We, however, must understand the people's motivations in this long-term process. I strongly believe that ego drives venture capitalists more than greed, but I want a little of both working for me all the time.

Glossary

AUDITED FINANCIALS Refer to carrying value.

CARRIED INTEREST The mechanism by which venture capitalist are compensated for their performance. The general partner's carried interest is his share of the partnership profits. Detailed definitions vary and are negotiable.

CARRYING VALUE A venture capital limited partner must list on its balance sheet a value for every investment it holds. These valuations are called the carrying values. The carrying values for individual companies are not audited; the auditor's letter always states that the audit was performed given those carrying values.

CASH-FLOW-POSITIVE COMPANY A company generating more cash then it consumes, making financing an option rather than a necessity.

CASH-ON-CASH RETURN The return to limited partners. Cash inflows are the capital calls of the partnership. Cash outflows are all distributions to the limited partners. Note that stock distributions are considered "cash" for this calculation.

CO-INVESTMENT RIGHTS A right, as defined by written agreement, for the named parties to invest alongside a particular venture capital fund.

COMMITTED CAPITAL When a venture capital limited partnership is formed, each limited partner agrees to contribute a certain amount of capital to the partnership. Once the agreement is signed, the dollar amount is said to be capital committed to the partnership.

CORPORATE INVESTOR An investor, in either a venture capital limited partnership or in a company, whose investment decision included strategic factors in addition to the usual financial return objective.

DISTRIBUTION PHASE Refers to limited partnerships that have ceased new investments and are distributing assets as they become liquid.

DOWN AND DIRTY FINANCING A round of investment where the stock price is substantially below the price of previous rounds. A new lead investor is almost always associated with down and dirty financing.

EXPANSION PHASE Refers to companies that are generating revenues and trying to expand those sales, usually rapidly.

GENERAL PARTNER As defined by the IRS code, the venture capitalists in a venture capital partnership.

GROSS IRR The return on the investments made by the partnership. Cash inflows are the investments in each company, on the dates of those investments. Outflows are the distributions of stock, plus the residual value of all stocks in the portfolio. Many variations exist, however, making apples-to-apples comparisons difficult without access to the data.

IN-KIND DISTRIBUTION When a venture partnership distributes stock of a public company to its investors.

J-CURVE Most venture partnerships go through their first few years with write-offs/downs exceeding write-ups, after which value increases rapidly as successful companies emerge. The plot of partnership value versus time, therefore, resembles a "J".

LATER STAGE FUND A venture capital fund that specializes in investing in (1) companies that already have revenues, or (2) companies that already have other venture capital investors.

LEAD INVESTOR The venture capital group responsible for assembling the investment syndicate is termed the lead investor. Under some circumstances, conflict of interest requires a different investor to establish the price of the round. The investor who establishes the price is then said to have "led the round."

LIMITED PARTNER As defined by the IRS code, any investor in a venture capital limited partnership.

LIQUIDATION PHASE Refers to limited partnerships nearing the end of their lives, where liquidating all investments becomes the priority.

LOOK-BACK PROVISION Carried interest provisions are imperfect, and often allocate more distributions to the general partner(s) than is due. The look-back, or make-up, provision provides a mechanism to remedy this deficit when the partnership is dissolved.

MAKE-UP PROVISION See look-back provision.

MANAGEMENT FEE Fee paid by the partnership to the general partner(s) for the ongoing management of the partnership.

MEZZANINE STAGE The last private round of financing before an anticipated public offering. Implies substantial revenues and usually the expectation of imminent profitability.

NET ASSET VALUE The difference between the assets and the liabilities, which can be calculated from the partnership's balance sheet.

NET ASSET VALUE BASED FEE A management fee that is calculated as a function of net asset value (NAV).

NET IRR Many definitions are available. When presented with a "net IRR," always ask for a detailed definition.

ORIGINATION A venture capitalist is said to have "originated the deal" if he (1) was the first venture capital investor, (2) worked with the company before a venture capital investment was made, or (3) structured the first round of venture capital financing.

PORTFOLIO FIRM Any of the companies in which a venture capital limited partnership has an investment are said to be in its portfolio (synonym portfolio company).

RESTORATION OF DEFICIT PROVISION See look-back provision.

ROUND OF INVESTMENT Venture capital-backed companies usually have several financings before they reach liquidity. Each such financing is termed a "round of investment" or "investment round."

SEED INVESTMENT Definitions vary, but seed deals are usually characterized by: an idea, no business plan, an incomplete or nonexistent management team, and a relatively small investment size.

SPECIALTY FUND A venture capital limited partnership that focuses on a specific type of business, for example biotechnology, specialty retailing, or advanced materials.

STAND ALONE FIRM A company with a satisfactory strategic position; a company that does not need to seek acquisition.

START-UP PHASE Definitions vary, but start-ups are usually characterized by: an initial business plan, a product that requires development, and a partially complete management team.

SYNDICATE Several venture capital partnerships may invest side by side in a given company. Such a group of venture capitalists is termed a syndicate. The art of bringing together such a group is termed syndication.

TAKE-DOWN/DRAW-DOWN Venture capital limited partnerships call their capital over a period of years in fractions of the total amount committed. Each such fraction may be termed a take-down, capital call, or tranche.

TIME AND ATTENTION CLAUSES A term included in limited partnership agreements that proscribe acceptable outside business interests for the general partner.

VENTURE CAPITALIST Someone who invests money and expertise in a portfolio of private companies with the hope of growing them rapidly and then liquidating the investments.

VENTURE PARTNERSHIP Short for venture capital limited partnership. A limited partnership, as defined by the IRS code, whose stated purpose is making venture capital investments.

Self-Evaluation Examination

1. According to Kane, the stage of venture investing that tends to require the largest infusion of funds is the:

    a. Start-up round.
    b. Seed investment stage.
    c. Expansion stage.
    d. Bridge financing stage.

2. The win-loss structure of venturing suggests that total or partial losses to a venture capital portfolio occur in about _____ of the companies owned:

    a. 10 percent
    b. 20 percent
    c. 40 percent
    d. 90 percent

3. The so-called "J-curve" in venture cycles refers to the:

    a. Call and distribution cycle.
    b. Partnership valuation cycle.
    c. Stock market exit cycle.
    d. Life cycle of portfolio companies.

4. According to French, venture capital returns:

    a. Outdistanced returns from large-capitalization stocks by about 900 basis points between 1977 and 1987.
    b. Were flat early and rising during the latter stages of the 1977-87 period.
    c. Will probably approach 20 to 25 percent per annum in the 1990s.
    d. Were higher over the period 1959-87 vs. the period 1977-87.

5. French suggests that venture capital returns in the future will tend to correlate:

    a. Negatively with non-dollar bonds.
    b. Less with bonds than with real estate.
    c. Positively with cash equivalents.
    d. At a level of about 0.75 with domestic equities.

6. Returns from venture investing tend *not* to be sensitive to:

    a. Take-down schedules.
    b. Timing and recognition of distributions.
    c. Valuations of underlying portfolio companies.
    d. Use of the internal rate of return measure.

7. According to Vincent, venture fund performance:

    a. Will be in the high teens, based on a poll of limited partners.
    b. Is facilitated by the presence of well over 40 years of meaningful historical data.
    c. Is best proxied by using the NASDAQ small-company stock index for the past 20 years.
    d. Is produced mostly by portfolio companies held for two to three years.

8. Private equity as an asset class is distinguished by:

    a. Near perfect markets.
    b. High expected returns and low expected risks.
    c. Illiquidity.
    d. Moderate expected returns and high expected risks.

9. According to Swensen, adding private equity to a portfolio of domestic stocks and bonds, real estate, and foreign stocks:

    a. Is not reasonable for endowment funds with their inherently short investment time horizons.
    b. Can add more than 100 basis points to returns for a given level of risk.
    c. Reduces portfolio risk because of the negative correlation between private equity and the other portfolio assets.
    d. Is effective because factors influencing public equities tend not to influence the private equity markets.

10. Marshall tells us that pension funds tend to view venture investing as:

    a. Inconsistent with the average life of their liabilities.
    b. Inappropriate in light of the high volatility inherent in pricing such assets.
    c. Perplexing under current fee structures because they relate to increasing fund size.
    d. Likely more rewarding in the future than during the period of the 1970s.

11. The institutionalization of venture investing has shown:

    a. Serious relaxation of the manner in which gains from such investing are taxed at the federal level.
    b. Increased interest on the part of public pension funds because portfolio managers are able to earn performance bonuses.
    c. Pressures on public pension funds to allocate venture allocations within their own states.
    d. Most very large pension funds find the pool of available venture investments of sufficient dollar size to permit a meaningful commitment of funds.

12. According to Landry, the major characteristics for success in a potential venture capital investment involve companies where:

    a. The president has great vision but lackluster management skills.
    b. The president is an outstanding manager but a mediocre visionary.
    c. The timing of entry into the market was poor but market growth was quite high.
    d. The board of directors was the critical element in the equation for success.

13. Landry would probably concur that successful venture capital investments are *not* usually found in:

    a. Companies with complete and proven management teams.
    b. The start-up stage because the price paid does not adequately compensate for the high risk assumed.
    c. Large, growing markets with limited number of competitors.
    d. Industries involved in technological products.

14. Johnson tells us that a good partnership is critical to the success of venture capital investments. Among the key characteristics of a partnership an investor should look for is:

    a. Decision making by each individual partner followed by pro forma approval at the partnership level.
    b. Whether the partnership uses a "big eight" CPA firm.
    c. Whether the partners will participate in active day-to-day management of portfolio companies.
    d. Whether the partnership has a strategy and adequate funding to carry the strategy forward.

15. Testa indicates that partnerships in venture investing:

    a. Are more likely to be a single limited partnership today rather than a two-tier partnership.
    b. Are extraordinarily efficient as business and tax vehicles when structured with a 10-year life.
    c. Are not the most effective arrangement for taxes and distribution of funds.
    d. Cannot survive when one focuses on the inefficiency of this management form.

16. Bliamptis indicates that the most significant detractor from the gross internal rate of return earned by limited partners is:

    a. The number of capital calls.
    b. Carried interest.
    c. Management fees.
    d. Accounting fees.

17. There are some terms of a partnership agreement that have indirect effects on the returns to limited partners. It is important to be on the lookout for:

    a. Formal co-investment rights that allow parties somehow related to the general partner to handpick the best investments.
    b. Lack of control on a general partner's right to start another fund prior to fulfilling obligations to existing funds.
    c. NAV-based fees which provide incentives of aggressive valuations.
    d. All of the above.

18. Pratt suggests that evaluations of current venturing opportunities do *not* include:

    a. Sufficient due diligence.
    b. Foreign firms as potential investments.
    c. More leveraged buyout deals.
    d. Corporate partnering.

19. Adams suggests that the supply of funds available for venturing has gone up about five to seven times faster than the amount of money actually invested in companies. This supply/demand imbalance:

    a. Tends to foster reneging on handshake agreements when a better deal (more money) can be found.
    b. Less trust and sharing of information.
    c. More of a hands-off approach (passive) after deals are done.
    d. All of the above.

20. A major trend in the future for venture investing, according to Adams, will likely be:

    a. Higher and more uniform returns across participants.
    b. Less effort to get out of funds.
    c. Desire for more frequent performance reporting, creating undue pressures to produce short-term results.
    d. Fund managers relying more on sharing gains than on management fee income.

Self-Evaluation Answers

See Kane:
    1) d
    2) c
    3) b

See French:
    4) a
    5) b
    6) d

See Vincent:
    7) a
    8) c

See Swensen:
    9) b

See Marshall:
    10) c
    11) c

See Landry:
    12) a
    13) b

See Johnson:
    14) d

See Testa:
    15) b

See Bliamptis:
    16) a
    17) d

See Pratt:
    18) a

See Adams:
    19) d
    20) c